Next to Nothing

Next to Nothing

A Theology from Outside

JAMES CHAMPION

CASCADE *Books* • Eugene, Oregon

NEXT TO NOTHING
A Theology from Outside

Copyright © 2024 James Champion. All rights reserved. Except for brief quotations in critical publications or reviews, no part of this book may be reproduced in any manner without prior written permission from the publisher. Write: Permissions, Wipf and Stock Publishers, 199 W. 8th Ave., Suite 3, Eugene, OR 97401.

Cascade Books
An Imprint of Wipf and Stock Publishers
199 W. 8th Ave., Suite 3
Eugene, OR 97401

www.wipfandstock.com

PAPERBACK ISBN: 978-1-6667-6888-6
HARDCOVER ISBN: 978-1-6667-6889-3
EBOOK ISBN: 978-1-6667-6890-9

Cataloguing-in-Publication data:

Names: Champion, James.

Title: Next to nothing : a theology from outside / James Champion.

Description: Eugene, OR : Cascade Books, 2024 | Includes bibliographical references and index.

Identifiers: ISBN 978-1-6667-6888-6 (paperback) | ISBN 978-1-6667-6889-3 (hardcover) | ISBN 978-1-6667-6890-9 (ebook)

Subjects: LCSH: Negative theology—Christianity. | Christianity—Philosophy.

Classification: BT83.585 .C43 2024 (print) | BT83.585 .C43 (ebook)

Scripture quotations are taken from New Revised Standard Version Bible, copyright 1989, National Council of Churches.

Excerpts from poems by Denise Levertov and William Carlos Williams are used with permission from New Directions Publishing Corporation, 80 Eighth Avenue, New York, NY 10011.

Excerpt from "Anthem" by Leonard Cohen is used with permission from The Wylie Agency, LLC, 250 W. 57th St., #2114, New York, NY 10107.

In memory of James Pearce Champion (1924–2017)

Table of Contents

Preface ix

Introduction xiii

Chapter One: An Apophatic Way 1

Chapter Two: On Knowing 10

Chapter Three: A Crack in Everything 21

Chapter Four: When the Light Gets In 48

Chapter Five: Kairos Calling 74

Conclusion 97

Bibliography 103

Index 113

Preface

THIS BOOK TRAFFICS IN abstractions, but it is rooted in concrete life. It arises out of study and teaching in the humanities, but it is born of personal experience. The personal aspect I want to mention here is my relationship with my father, who passed away in 2017. This book is dedicated to him because, from an early age, he initiated my wonder about the world.

If you got to know my father, he might well have told you about a time when everything changed for him. It happened on a Tuesday. That would be Tuesday, June 6, 1944.

The Canadian soldiers who jumped out of landing craft, at Normandy, France, that day made their way, in terror, to shore. Landing crafts were hitting mines. My father said that he found himself, at one absurd moment, carrying someone unconscious. He said "it was so loud you couldn't think." At another point, he found himself completely under water when a wave surged over him. Sometimes he would simply describe the nightmare of that long day as "chaos."

My father had gone into the war as a devout Christian Scientist. If there was a free moment, he would be off reading his Mary Baker Eddy, while other men were doing other things. But his Christian Science belief system deserted him at Normandy. He found himself, in his fear, in prayer, bargaining with God for his life. He had enough presence of mind to catch himself doing this— and in that moment, he realized that his Christian Science beliefs were based in illusion.

Preface

People react in different ways to the loss of their belief systems. Some get angry and erect a counter-belief system that mirrors the rigidity of the one they escaped. Some people find integrity simply in standing, with courage, against dominant dehumanizing worldviews. And then there are those who double down and repress their doubt, and, because they are repressing their own fears of being wrong, they assume they have the right to suppress doubts in everyone else too. Others react to the loss of their belief system by building a fortress of cynicism. I don't mean the humane kind wherein to be cynical is, often, simply to be true to life. I mean the cynicism that's really a defense. It makes sure you never get opened up to the unsure things that can break your heart, and it can do the job efficiently and for no less than a lifetime.

The way my father dealt with the loss of his belief system was unusual, somehow. I think it had a lot to do with his concern and his open way of relating to others, and it's what I'm trying to get at here.

After the war, my father worked at the Vancouver Fire Department. Through the Veteran's Land Act in Canada, my parents bought a parcel of land down a dirt road. Over time, my father built two houses there. With my sisters and brother (and a few animals), we grew up on this land that was next to a post-war, cookie-cutter housing development. When friends from school were allowed to make it over to our neck of the woods, they would sometimes remark on the way you could talk about things around our place. When my father was part of these conversations, he would sometimes play the role of devil's advocate. If he sensed you were getting too narrow in your, let's say, political beliefs, he was inclined to say, characteristically, "well, there's another way of looking at things." When you absolutely knew you were totally right, this could be really aggravating. My father too would, of course, hold strong positions lots of times, and I don't mean to idealize his penchant for viewing other sides of things. But there was also something distinctive in his way of doing this. It affected me in ways I didn't understand until later on.

Preface

When I first tried to go to university, I was ill-prepared and had to withdraw. When I went the second time, attending Simon Fraser University, I found myself learning a lot from two teachers in particular. They were very different in their approaches. I think they even disliked being in the same room together. But I found myself thinking they were both right, and I worked on trying to put it all together. I think the inclination to do so came from my father.

When I went to Emory University, I had to defend my dissertation in both written and oral exams. I had written on Paul Ricoeur's notion that you can be both suspicious and receptive in the act of interpretation, which I applied to three authors: George Eliot, William Faulkner, and Denise Levertov (with constant reference to Herman Melville). I can't remember exactly what I was grilled on the day of my oral exam, but I do recall that when I walked into the room to face my four interrogators, it hit me: I got this idea from my dad.

To return to my early years, I remember one day when I was talking with my father at the kitchen table, and the D-Day scenario came up. I found myself reversing roles—for fun, initially. Playing devil's advocate, I said, "Well, maybe your prayer was answered that day. Just not in the way you expected." We both had a bit of a laugh at this. He smiled and said, "Yeah, my mom used to say, 'Jimmy, God was protecting you that day.'" Well, we both knew that wasn't true, and, I realized after, that isn't what I meant. We both knew there is no supernatural being in the sky picking this person to live, and that person to, say, get blown to pieces. Things in this world do not transpire supernaturally. Chance isn't circumvented because you want it to be. If the laws of nature were breached for one second or a single atom, the very structure of life, not to mention the universe, would disappear. But because nothing supernatural occurs, it doesn't mean the world isn't deep. And sometimes you get thrown into a depth you don't control. Sometimes you see things you couldn't see before. Sometimes you realize answers appear when discerned in an unexpected way. It's like that story of the ancient Hebrew teacher, Hillel. Hated by the dogmatists of his day, they mocked him by challenging him to stand on one leg and to recite the entire Torah. When he stood on one leg and uttered the golden rule, calling the rest "commentary," it was not the answer they were expecting.

I think my father lost his belief system, and then he encountered his life at a different level in his remaining years. I think that concern with something that matters, the passion that underpinned his Christian Science years, dropped down deep. In a way, it resurfaced, though. It resurfaced in his adherence to what he understood to be the golden rule, though he never made a big show of this.

I remember my father was glad when he learned that the golden rule can be found all over the planet. First coined by Confucius with a negative twist—do not do to others what you would not do to yourself—you can find versions of it in religions and cultures in many times and places. I remember occasions when we were watching the news on TV, and, when it was especially awful, my father might ask out loud, with some exasperation, "What's the matter with man?" If there is any answer, I think he had decided some version of the golden rule was about the only way out. I have never known anyone who did so many things for other people.

My father came home from the war. My gratitude to him and my love for him will always be more than I can possibly say. I know I will continue to wonder about his prayer that day. I know it's just another way of looking at things.

Introduction

The cradle rocks above an abyss, and common sense tells us that our existence is but a brief crack of light between two eternities of darkness. —Nabokov[1]

We're all going to die, all of us, what a circus! That alone should make us love each other, but it doesn't. We are terrorized and flattened by trivialities.... —Bukowski[2]

WE ARE NOT IN this life long, and soon we will be forever gone. As we get older, it becomes obvious we don't have long. But can we really grasp the *forever* part? Likely not, for even after we realize that the universe will be able to get along without us—admittedly, a tough call—we are always somewhere having the realization. In our minds, we are still here even when we imagine ourselves gone.

To think about these things isn't morbid. Moreover, to avoid them may amount to an everyday form of craziness. Death matters because our deep anxiety about it determines so much. But it's hard to see our anxiety—maybe *dread* is a better word—for it lies below the surface of our everyday interactions. Nevertheless, it's possible to bring it into focus. In the discussion that follows, I will try to face it by starting with an observation of Philip Roth's: "In

---

1. Nabokov, *Speak, Memory*, 9.
2. Bukowski, *Captain Is Out to Lunch*, 7.

every calm and reasonable person there is a hidden second person scared witless about death."³

Many people see how Roth's claim might apply to religious folk. After all, isn't religion basically underwritten by the universal fear of having to die? From this view, religious masses the world over hold fast to the idea that they are not destined to extinction. Their souls will survive the death of the body, and given their worthy actions and beliefs in their time on earth, they will, in effect, ascend to some sort of heavenly or nirvanic state. Both the despisers of religion and the authoritarians within religion assume this is the upshot of religion. But where the critics of this belief know it's a collective lie, the fundamentalists within religion tend to highlight it as the reason for having faith in the first place.

Fundamentalists the world over believe you don't actually die. Some are humble when anticipating their afterlives, while others do not hesitate to mix worldly impulses into their upcoming bliss. For example, an Islamic terrorist may blow up other humans, but, as a martyr, he can expect to retain ninety-two virgins in heaven for his trouble. Many American evangelical Christians picture themselves reunited with their families in a heavenly paradise, but they will also be well placed to witness the misery of the damned who won't make it.

Whether one is for or against the fundamentalist take on religion, the problem is that it is monumentally reductive. From this angle, religion has only one access point: the literal. Before turning to a broader and deeper understanding of religion, though, consider how the fear of death plays out in secular world views too.

It was Ernest Becker, in his Pulitzer-Prize-winning book, *The Denial of Death* (1973), who showed how human culture, in both its sacred and secular permutations, works to alleviate our awareness of our inevitable demise. The religious may have their afterlives, but the nonreligious and the anti-religious have their own means for dispensing with awareness of death, even if the solace thereby gained is less explicit. Secular roles in modern cultures provide templates for living out normal or heroically good lives. Thereby

3. Roth, *Dying Animal*, 153.

INTRODUCTION

they provide meaning that serves a host of *social* ends—but such meaning also serves the *psychological* end of mitigating the dread of knowing that, soon enough, we will all be permanently gone. In Becker's terms, "It doesn't matter whether the cultural hero-system is frankly magical, religious, and primitive or secular, scientific, and civilized. It is still a mythical hero-system in which people serve in order to earn a feeling of primary value, of cosmic specialness, of ultimate usefulness to creation, of unshakable meaning."[4]

Many modern people have the courage to reject religion. They are sure it's a mental crutch. They are honest enough to admit it's false for them. What's often left out of the picture, though, is that such honesty and courage are doing more work than meets the eye. They also buffer against our nothingness by providing sources of self-esteem. In other words, a purely secular scheme of things, no less than a devoutly religious one, depends on self-images and cultural narratives that foster and sustain our sense that our lives really matter. Having offspring, doing good works, contributing to science, and getting a building erected in your name can serve this end.

Things go awry, however, when the threat of nothingness reels too immediately into view. The pillars of our world views shake when natural disasters, wars, fatal accidents, lethal illness, or, say, unanticipated neighborhood killings startle us into remembering that the inevitable endpoint can arrive at any time. When we are shocked into facing what's threatening and beyond our control, we may be prompted into heroic action; however, our behavioral norms can take abrupt negative turns as well. As George Bernard Shaw once put it, "When the angel of death sounds his trumpet the pretenses of civilization are blown from men's heads into the mud like hats in a gust of wind."[5]

Like all forms of life, human beings are biologically predisposed towards self-preservation. But our evolutionary brain development, from reptilian stem to limbic layer to cerebral cortex, also makes us conscious, for better or worse, that we are ephemeral

---

4. Becker, *Denial of Death*, 5.
5. Shaw, *Heartbreak House*, 34.

creatures through and through. "All people are grass," is one way to say it.

That "grass" metaphor is found in the Hebrew Bible in the book of Isaiah (40:6–7). It's an ancient expression about the human condition. I want to place it here as a kind of marker, a remonstrance, if you will, against the tendency to simply equate religion with a childish longing for heaven, with a mentality, in other words, best outgrown, lest it impede progress. All religion is not necessarily deluded about death or anti-scientific in what it knows. The history of religion is complicated and diverse; it has multiple voices and layers, including realistic streams of thought. "You are dust and dust you shall be" (Gen 3:19), for example, is not the sort of uplifting utterance you would expect from an imaginary friend.

Speaking of God, God would seem to be a fitting place to start when dealing with the contours of religion—Western religion, at least. When the Canadian philosopher Charles Taylor published his influential book *A Secular Age* in 2007, he opened this 800-page study with a question: "Why was it virtually impossible not to believe in God in, say, 1500 in our Western society, while in 2000 many of us find this not only easy but even inescapable?"[6] To attempt to answer this question is to tell a long story, including one's interpretive takes on key developments such as Renaissance humanism, Protestantism, the scientific revolution, Deism, the Enlightenment, Romanticism, liberal theology, atheism, and neo-orthodoxy, not to mention numerous interrelated social, artistic, political, and economic transformations.

For the purposes of brevity here, a different approach can be taken, namely, through *ontology*. Ontology, the branch of philosophy focused on the knowledge of being, is often viewed as inferior to *epistemology*, the knowledge of knowing. British analytic philosophy in particular, the dominant school in North America, has tended to dismiss ontology as "mere metaphysics," thereby tagging ontology as unrealistic. Hoping to attain the status of a science, analytic philosophy restricts itself to questions of language and

---

6. Taylor, *Secular Age*, 25.

Introduction

correct epistemological propositions. But it's possible to fight back against such narrowness. In short, it is possible to treat knowing as an event within the totality of events and to focus instead on descriptions of the world and what it is like to be alive.[7] From this angle of vision, developed in the twentieth century through the movements of existentialism and phenomenology, epistemology becomes secondary to ontology. Everything human then comes into view, from our innate wonder to our deepest fears, without reducing cognitive truth to sterile propositions or explaining it away as a mere biochemical reaction in the brain.

A key insight arising from the field of ontology is that when it comes to religion, the modern world is marked by a distinctive shift. This shift, driven from fundamentalism, is a turn from understanding God as *being itself* to the treatment of God as literally *a being*. In the twentieth century, it was Paul Tillich, above all, who woke up many to the ways in which modern religious literalism had supplanted the notion of God as being itself by turning God into an object among objects, a very large, supernatural object at that. This development has generated two dominant postures in its wake, and they frame much contemporary talk about religion: on the one hand, the position of those who summon the will to believe that the supernatural entity, God, exists; and, on the other hand, the stance of those who are not fooled by any such claim, namely the repudiation and disavowals of atheism.

For its capacity to illuminate issues in religion, I will be returning throughout this study to further points drawn from ontology. Pertinent to the point with which I began, for instance, ontology can provide insight into death as an irrevocable factor in our lives. It's the human condition. We are in it all the time. From an ontological perspective, we can delineate human life succinctly as *finite freedom*. "Freedom" here refers to the intrinsic potential of self-consciousness; human beings have some capacity to choose,

---

7. Tillich, *Systematic Theology*, 1:71. The same point is made by David Walsh in *Modern Philosophical Revolution*. As Walsh puts it, the decisive step in this modern philosophical turn comes with "recognizing that knowledge is a mode of being, not a holding of being at a distance in the act of contemplation" (18).

however minimal, and to act on the basis of those choices. On the other hand, we are never not finite. We are limited in our choices and actions by the fact that we will die. This unremitting hitch flies in the face of those who fantasize that technological breakthroughs will one day make us immortal. It's also an affront to those who explain everything human as a function of social construction. For example, the social sciences may show that what we call "human nature" is in many respects conditioned and determined by ideological, economic, and cultural forces, and, as these forces change, human nature may well change too. Briefly put, human nature changes in history. But that presupposes that nature of a creature that *can have history* to begin with.[8] In other words, it presupposes at least some ontological stipulations about what constitutes human life, whether these are hidden, divulged, or postponed for later consideration.

Immense human creativity unfolds in history. But so does our propensity for slaughter. "Finite freedom" is an abstract formulation. Human genocide, on the other hand, is all too concrete. If Becker is right, under normal circumstances, the repression of our finitude (i.e., death) awareness enables us to function smoothly enough within the belief systems provided by our cultures. But what about the very different belief systems in other cultures? According to Becker, hostility towards the other is triggered at an unconscious level when we encounter contrary belief systems.[9] For if "those people" are right about human life, maybe we are not. Besides, why do those people seem to be against us? Especially in times of crisis, our limitations loom and fissures in our walls appear. Blind spots in our defenses become more difficult to ignore. Hatred of other races, nations, and religions normalizes. Scapegoating of the other escalates. Historically speaking, the killing of innocent people and the collective madness of war are seldom far

---

8. Tillich, *Systematic Theology*, 1:167.

9. This aspect of Becker's thought is explained by Solomon et al., *In the Wake of 9/11*. See also Solomon et al., *Worm at the Core*.

INTRODUCTION

behind. In short, human creativity may unfold in history, but as Georg Hegel once put it, history is a veritable "butcher's bench."[10] When Hegel used this startling image, he was taking a momentary break from trafficking in pure concepts. The image is hard to forget, and it conveys even more than Hegel could have known. The industrialized carnage of World War I, for example, was yet around the historical corner. Such is the power of images and analogies. Along with metaphors and symbols, they express facets of the human predicament that can make abstract language seem anemic by comparison.

To return to an earlier example, God may mean *being itself* at the level of philosophical abstraction. But that's not the idiom people praying in dire straits use. Father, Mother, Savior, Fortress, etc., are metaphors more likely at hand. There are persons in all the world religions—practitioners for whom doubt and questioning are elements of faith and not the opposite of faith—who can use such language in awareness of its metaphorical aspect. Fundamentalists, on the other hand, do not; they reject the idea that their creeds are replete with figurative language, for to acknowledge as much would interfere with doctrinal certainty, not to mention the need to weaponize select scriptural passages. Yet a third position towards religious metaphors is that of anti-religious folk. They too take the metaphors as literal, which leads naturally to the rejection of such talk as magical thinking and to the inference that religion itself is simply passé.

The kind of knowledge intrinsic to metaphor, symbol, and myth will be discussed in chapter 2. In closing these introductory remarks, I wish to note what is at stake in the meaning of religious language and why the spiritual dimension of life warrants critical understanding. Religion's complicity in xenophobia, racism, colonialism, and patriarchal oppression underwrites wars that take up a lot of space on Hegel's bench. But the violence born of authoritarian religion will not be defused by dismissing all religion as passé. As the modern secularized world dispenses with the sacred, the human capacity for fear, egotism, and greed appears unlikely

---

10. Hegel, *Philosophy of History*, 21.

to fade. From the guillotining craze that surged when the French Revolution enthroned Reason, to the atheism of Stalin, Hitler, Mao, and Pol Pot—no slouches when it comes to exterminating millions—scorn for religious transcendence, or what Trotsky called "prattle about the sacredness of human life,"[11] doesn't alleviate atrocity. However counterintuitive it may seem to those who reject talk of religion outright, struggles against despotism and injustice today may find surprising resources for countering violence in dialogue with nonfundamentalist persons of faith the world over.

Ernest Becker was fond of quoting Thomas Hardy to the effect that "if a way to the better there be, it lies in taking a full look at the worst."[12] The worst is that our anxiety of death provokes lethal adherence to fixed doctrines. Ways to the better could take the form of cultural and religious practices that made it possible for most people to find the value and meaning that make up self-esteem—without creating scapegoats, impoverished classes, or resident hate objects. Ways to the better would have an outside chance in a culture that acknowledges the unknown, the uncanny, and our proximity to *no-thing-ness*. Ways to the better could thrive in a culture that permitted reinterpretation of its own symbols, a culture of spiritual depth that would not disguise the "fear of death behind our normal functioning."[13] Dag Hammarskjöld, the religious head of the United Nations after World War II, who, in his work as a peace activist, died tragically in a plane crash in 1961, was no supernaturalist intent on getting to heaven. His religious standpoint, expressed in his remarkable book of reflections, *Markings*, led him to speak of "the point of rest at the center of our being."[14] Perhaps such a center is indigenous to our psyche. The venture that leads to its rediscovery can expand our experience of the richness and urgency of what it means to be alive.

11. Quoted in Osborn, *Humanism and the Death of God*, 105.
12. Becker, *Escape from Evil*, ix.
13. Becker, *Denial of Death*, 16.
14. Hammarskjold, *Markings*, 174.

Chapter One: An Apophatic Way

Already have we been the nothing we dread to be. —Herman Melville[1]

In the beginning is the relation. —Martin Buber[2]

Let us pray to God that we may be free of "God." —Meister Eckhart[3]

JOHN LENNON'S WELL-KNOWN SONG, "Imagine" (1971), contains latent religious ideas. The summons to imagine a world without religion makes the song, for many, a kind of atheist anthem. Yet the lyrics have biblical antecedents. Whether Lennon picked these up in childhood, or by osmosis at the church event where he first met Paul McCartney, is anybody's guess.[4] In any case, anyone familiar with the ancient beatitude, "Blessed are the peacemakers" (Matt 5:9), could be forgiven if she or he heard an echo in the song's global call to live life peacefully. The idea that there will be an end to religion is found, surprisingly, in the phantasmagoric book of Revelation, with its vision of a fulfilled future in which there is no temple (Rev 21:22). A precedent for giving up all possessions appears in the New Testament book of Acts. As reported by the Gospel writer Luke, the earliest Christians "would sell their

1. Melville, *Mardi*, 237.
2. Buber, *I and Thou*, 69.
3. Eckhart, *Eckhart: The Essential Sermons*, 200. See also Sells, *Mystical Languages of Unsaying*, 1.
4. See Holland, *Dominion*, 492 and 496.

possessions and goods and distribute the proceeds to all, as any had need" (Acts 2:45). In this original community, "no one claimed private ownership of any possessions, but everything they owned was held in common" (Acts 4:32). It was a radical stance, while it lasted, and it has been emulated by dissenting groups throughout history in the ongoing struggle to combat the corruption and calcification of the established, hierarchy-obsessed church. A small group, the Diggers, for example, made a run at ground-breaking egalitarianism in 1649 when they occupied St. Georges Hill—an area of London where Lennon, ironically enough, would come to buy a large home—hoping at the time that others would join their movement to share all the world.

The point of these remarks is that secular and religious ideas are historically interrelated. The dialectic between them can be annoying for both true believers and nonbelievers who prefer their own side uncontaminated by the other. Religious incentives sometimes further secular aims. For example, in the ancient Mediterranean world, Gal 3:28 envisioned life beyond the binaries of slave and free, Jew and Greek, and male and female. At the dawning of the nation of America, it was the Pilgrims who first stood for the separation of church and state, however much right-wing evangelicals have betrayed that notion through recent power grabs. On the other hand, secular movements have repeatedly awakened religious communities to the demand for social justice, a sacred mandate that institutionalized religion repeatedly betrays.

The struggle for social justice in the Western world is rooted in the Jewish prophetic tradition. The Hebrew scriptures contain creation stories, poems, tribal legends, and wisdom sayings paralleled in other ancient middle eastern religions. But the prophetic writings are distinctive. The historical context that gave rise to figures such as Amos, Isaiah, and Jeremiah is not entirely clear. Did the catastrophe of exile and loss of land prompt an elevation of time over space in Hebrew self-understanding? Did ancient Israel's clash with space-bound gods lead to covenant with a deity who, untied to space, brings a new heaven and new earth? In any case, the prophets' rebukes of idolatry and their calls to free

Chapter One: An Apophatic Way

the oppressed and protect the poor presume a new vision of what should be. Their indictments are not sanctioned soothsaying.[5] The warnings, which lead to ostracization, are not divinations of already set events. They stem from a full-frontal view of corruption in the *present* time. The prophets point out pending destruction because they see what complacency towards injustice is bound to bring.

The stance of the prophets may seem strange to us today, yet you can hear it reverberating in voices in the modern world too. In Martin Luther King's "I Have a Dream" speech (1963), for example, it's not an accident that we find the book of Amos (5:24) quoted: "we will not be satisfied until justice rolls down like waters and righteousness like a mighty stream." Like Amos, King feels called to expose injustice. Like the ancient Hebrews, who thought their people had been redeemed from slavery (see Exodus), King indicts "the manacles of segregation and the chains of discrimination" that amount to "a shameful condition" in the nation. He is addressing the nation as a religious witness in "the fierce urgency of now."[6] These are not words that bedeck secular hopes in pious garb. I wish to emphasize this point here because I think that exclusive secularity, in its fight against the oppressiveness of religion, should not lose sight of these prophetic roots. Differently put, don't throw out the humanist baby with the biblical bathwater.

One way to deal with the oppressiveness of religion is to ignore religion. Another way is to get beyond religion by going *through* religion. When it comes to the Bible, many people equate the Bible with the fundamentalist view of it, namely, that it is consistent with itself. It has one meaning which you submit to or you don't. Bible debunkers, uncovering ideology and howlers, duplicate this univocal approach. Such hidebound reading, however, ignores studies and commentaries from within the world of religion that are attuned to criticism and to polyvocality. The practice of midrash, for example, seeks multiple meanings in sacred texts, while regarding gaps in stories as invitations to interpretation. The overarching

5. Heschel, *Prophets*, 16.
6. King, "I Have a Dream," 625–28.

picture, as Timothy Beal notes, is that the Bible "is a cacophony of voices and perspectives, often in conflict with one another. . . . Biblical literature is constantly interpreting, interrogating, and disagreeing with itself. Virtually nothing is asserted someplace that is not called into question or undermined elsewhere." For example, one psalmist proclaims assurance about God's world, while another sees chaos and divine absence. Beal goes on to say that "ultimately [the Bible] resists conclusion and explodes any desire we might have for univocality."[7] The upshot is that biblical literacy is a real thing, and it should start with awareness that the Bible was thousands of years in the making. In it you will find toxic age-old edicts amidst emancipatory ideas aborning. Within the very first pages of Genesis, you can read two different creation stories written hundreds of years apart. And while in Genesis, why not notice that the Hebrew flood story was derived from Babylonian mythology, before it was given an ethical twist. Or, if turning to the New Testament, why not be aware at the outset that, in the ancient Roman police state, more than one author was writing in the name of "Paul," and, moreover, that the writers of the New Testament stories—composed over decades with a view to the needs and situations of the communities that received them—intended nothing like newspaper accounts. Finally, why not remain open to surprise and discover that the Bible includes a humorous sendup of the call to prophecy (book of Jonah), an analysis of the human condition that would do Samuel Beckett proud (Ecclesiastes), and a celebration of the power and joy of erotic love (Song of Songs)?

To repeat, one way to dispense with soul-sapping religion is to airbrush all reference to religion out of the picture. But another way is to get beyond religion by going through it, more specifically, through its marginalized resources. One of those resources is apophatic theology.

I am aware that "theology," for many, is a word beyond the pale. Nowadays the term comes so laden with associations of bigotry and arrogance, it may be beyond recovery. In my own experience, its mere mention can prompt bemused incredulity:

---

7. Beal, "Bible is Dead," B6–B8.

Chapter One: An Apophatic Way

"you mean you want to talk about how many angels can dance on the head of a pin?" Actually, no. I watch an anti-science evangelist hawking snake-oil "prayer-products" on TV—complete with references to the Bible and "theology" in his ad—and I am ready to dispense with the word. Nevertheless, my hope for an outside chance of retrieval returns. I remember other words whose connotations seemed beyond recoupment. For example, when I first moved to the US in the 1980s, I soon learned that I would do well not to say that I am a socialist. For before I could add the qualifier "democratic," the rejoinder came quick: "You want the government to run everything? You mean you don't believe in freedom?" In recent years, however, especially in the wake of rampant income inequality and the devastation it has wrought, the term "democratic socialism" has found some renewal.[8] In short, the following discussion assumes that sometimes a word or term can find its way towards new discernment.

"Theology" is a compound composed of two Greek words. In its most basic sense, it means language or thought (*logos*) about God (*theos*)—where, I hasten to add, God means *being itself*, not *a* being. In its broadest conception, it involves study of religious truth and experience, but the idea that this entails a denial of scientific truth is false.

The dominant kind of theology is *cataphatic*. Being itself is not an entity, and therefore, not finally knowable as a thing, but that doesn't stop theologians of the cataphatic persuasion from attempting to refer to God's attributes, and then universalizing the terms of divine presence. From this angle—the *via affirmativa* of Western Christendom—human reason, while limited, enables us to know God's transcendent reality. Doctrines follow. Theological systems are constructed as needed.

In contrast to cataphatic systems that confidently name God as starting point, *apophatic* theology is at pains to say what God is *not*. At one level, it is an assault on the hubris of presuming that

---

8. For an analysis of the rise of poverty, addiction, and suicide stemming from income inequality, see Case and Deaton, *Deaths of Despair and the Future of Capitalism*.

humans can control everything. As a species of negative theology—the *via negativa*—it begins by denying "all descriptions and attributes as predicated of God."[9] This places it in the paradoxical position of using words to deny that what transcends us can be named. The relation between finite creature and the infinite—from which we come and to which we return—remains a mystery that is unsayable, though we strive to comprehend it.

Cataphatic theologians are not exactly popular household names, but some people have at least heard of, say, St. Augustine (ancient world), Thomas Aquinas (medieval world), or Karl Barth (modern world). But the apophatic types are largely unknown. That's because such thinking has long remained an undercurrent in Western religious thought. Authoritarians and power brokers in Western Christendom have long propounded a triumphalist theology of established dogmas because it more directly serves the institutions of entrenched orthodoxy.

In the undercurrent world of apophatic theology, by contrast, one finds more obscure figures, such as Marguerite Porete, Nicholas of Cusa, and Meister Eckhart, not to mention anonymous works such as *The Cloud of Unknowing*. This alternative tradition sometimes deconstructs rigid ideas, including official conceptions of God. It's hard to miss this impulse in the Dominican scholar Meister Eckhart (1260–1328) who, in a sermon in Cologne, prayed to God "to rid us of 'God.'" Eckhart's contention that "the eye by which I see God is the same with which God sees me"[10] further deconstructs the idea of God as a detached, condemning observer. Eckhart believed that all human beings are equally gifted in the core of their souls. His aid to the Beguines (lay women mystics and monastics) was particularly disturbing to the patriarchal hierarchs of his day.

One way the apophatic angle on religious meaning matters today is in providing a gateway for communication between world religions. For example, William Franke's breakthrough work,

---

9. Franke, *On What Cannot Be Said: Apophatic Discourses*, 1:1.

10. Eckhart, *Meister Eckhart: An Introduction and an Anthology*, Sermon XX, 227.

Chapter One: An Apophatic Way

Apophatic Paths from Europe to China: Regions without Borders, explores differences and similarities between Eastern and Western expressions of the unfathomability of ultimate reality. In other words, what might Lao Tzu's eternal *Dao*—the Dao "which cannot be spoken"—have to do with the *Ein Sof* in Kabbalistic Judaism? Or how does the Buddhist notion of Sunyata relate to the metaphor of God as the "ground" of being and non-being? The point is not that these and other traditions are all saying the same thing. Rather, because apophatic thinking integrates the factor of unknowability from the very start, the compulsion to defend impervious belief systems recedes. Open-ended dialogue—however much fundamentalists may try to quash it—can become a cross-cultural and cross-religious touchstone. In his book *The Religious Case Against Belief*, James Carse has written that "to be human at all is to live in an ill-lit zone of imponderables: *Why am I alive at all? Where did I come from and where am I going? . . . Why must so much of the world live in misery and violence? Why such collective self-destruction? Why do the evil prosper? Why is there something rather than nothing?*"[11] The experience of loss—the shock of non-being—that gives rise to such questions is apophatic through and through. But it is the common humanity in our responses, not this name or that name, that finally matters for our engagement with the world and the sacred dimension of life.

While the word "apophatic" derives from theology, I think it can be conceptionally expanded to signify an approach to the world that gives the negative its due. Giving the negative its due means, first of all, acknowledging our finitude. We contain our end within ourselves. To use ontological terms again, we are never not a mixture of being and non-being. We come from and return to *no-thing-ness*. To try to face this predicament is not grandiose; we don't solve the problem of death or change human nature. It means simply that we may thereby become less susceptible to immortality ideologies and toxic tribalism. Becoming more cognizant of the death anxiety that looms in our own belief systems, secular and religious, can help us let go of our own in-group bias—the script

---

11. Carse, *Religious Case Against Belief*, 159–60.

we cling to for dear life—and inspire us to stand up for tolerance and for the just treatment of others.[12]

Religion scholar Karen Armstrong has noted that just as we need to understand our relationship to fellow humans and to our economic and historical situation, we also need to see "our relationship to nothingness. To death."[13] However strange it is to utter, if we come from nothingness and return to nothingness, aren't we in some way in relationship to nothingness? I realize that for many people today, this is not something to waste time thinking about. The point is to get on with enjoying your life while you are here. And so what anyway? Maybe our lives can be compared to drops of water: for a brief time, we are separated from the ocean from which we come and to which we return. There's no particular meaning to it all.

On the other hand, throughout the long history of human cultures, others have understood this relationship in a different way. They have practiced rituals, formed commonwealth communities, and created works of art that embody their understanding, and they have used symbol, metaphor, and myth to express it. They feel called to look beyond "the veil of triviality."[14] They are guided by the intuition that life is a gift. They sense that the unfathomable beauty of the world calls for response. In the face of unrelenting loss, they seek mercy. When mercy comes, it brings healing that enters our lives as physically as oxygen enters our lungs and combines with the blood in our veins.

Simone Weil, a contemporary of Jean Paul Sartre and Simone de Beauvoir, speaks directly to the idea that we are more than a random assortment of atoms. She writes, "At the heart of every human being, from earliest infancy until the tomb, there is something that goes on indomitably expecting, in the teeth of crimes

---

12. This has been the task of the Ernest Becker Foundation as it sought to support research emphasizing the values of tolerance and common humanity to reduce defensive behavior in the face of mortality. See www.ernestbecker.org.

13. Armstrong, *Fields of Blood*, 400. Armstrong is quoting novelist John Fowles, *Magus*, 413.

14. Sölle, *Silent Cry*, 89.

committed, suffered, and witnessed, that good and not evil will be done to him." Weil goes on to say that "it is this above all that is sacred in every human being."[15] The kind of knowledge entailed in such a claim and the issues of the heart underwriting it are the subject of the following chapter.

---

15. Weil, "Human Personality," 315.

Chapter Two: On Knowing

> Regarding religion as an attempt to offer a scientific explanation of the world... is rather like seeing a ballet as a botched attempt to run for a bus. —Terry Eagleton[1]
>
> And then a Plank in Reason, broke,
> And I dropped down, and down
> —Emily Dickinson[2]

THERE ARE TWO KINDS of knowledge. One kind is not better than the other—they're just different. The overarching point is that some human activities that entail knowing aren't concerned foremostly with facts. For example, if you are dealing with a work of art, or a religious symbol, or a fictional narrative, or a poem, or a film, or a sculpture, or any kind of cultural creation for that matter, you are called upon to interpret too. To add further examples, if you're trying to understand the meaning of an historical event or attempting to discern the significance of a human life—perhaps someone you have known who has passed away—factual information isn't your only clue. Rather, you are engaged with a type of thinking that has its own ends, and it's not the same order of business as data determination.

---

1. Eagleton, *Faith, Reason, and Revolution*, 12.
2. Dickinson, *Final Harvest*, 43.

Chapter Two: On Knowing

One way to explain the distinction is by differentiating between *receiving knowledge* and *controlling knowledge*.³ Philosophy helps here—more specifically, the age-old tradition in philosophy of defining knowledge in general as *the coming together of subject and object*. In other words, in every act of knowing, there is a union of a person (a human subject) with some particular thing (an object).

In the case of controlling knowledge, there is a coming together of subject and object for the sake of control of the object by the subject. Tremendous amounts of technical information can be derived in this way. Along with freeing us from superstitions, there are a vast number of concrete uses to which this objective information can be applied. Moreover, there is a very reliable means for determining whether something counts as objectively factual or not, namely *experiment*. You have to be able to repeat a discovery in a demonstration or experiment—one showing the labor-saving functionality of a pulley, say, or the structure of the DNA molecule, to give a more complex example—in order to claim it counts as knowledge.

In the case of receiving knowledge, there is a coming together of subject and object, but it's for the sake of the union, not necessarily for some use to which it can be put. For example, if you find yourself responding to a song downloaded on your phone, or playing on the radio, or on a refurbished turntable, and you really *know* that song, you know it in a way that's different from grasping the technical information (analogue or digital) that enabled it to be transmitted to your ears.

If the means of verification in controlling knowledge is *experiment*, the means of verification in receiving knowledge is *experience*. It is experiential in the sense that it relates to the whole

---

3. These terms are derived from Paul Tillich's treatment of different kinds of reason in *Systematic Theology*, 1:72–75, 81–83, and 97–103. There are family resemblances between the different terms used by modern thinkers to differentiate between subjective and objective modes of thinking. For example, Michael Polanyi uses the term *tacit knowing* in his critique of mechanistic positivism, and Max Horkheimer and Theodor Adorno use the term *instrumental reason* for what Tillich calls technical reason.

person, and in relating to the whole person it entails ontological reason, as opposed to technical reason.

With receiving knowledge, the means of verification may include emotion, although it doesn't have to. This places it outside the realm of experimental verification, where human emotion should not be involved. Differently put, if you read an article in *Scientific American*, you don't expect to hear about how the author's personal feelings entered into the collection of data. On the other hand, if you find yourself responding to a parable, a novel, a photograph, a musical composition, a painting, a movie, a scriptural passage, a concert, a dance performance, a play, etc., your feeling is not at that moment disassociated from what you know.

In the modern world, there has been an astonishing explosion of controlling knowledge and technical reason. At the dawn of the modern world, when the traditional authorities of received knowledge caught a glimpse of the power of this kind of reason, they tried to suppress it. For example, when Galileo looked through his telescope and saw that, no, actually the sun did not revolve around the earth, he was thrown in jail and ordered to recant.

Perhaps we now live in a time when things have reversed. That is, maybe in our day the kind of information that can be gained through the calculating power of technical reason has become so dominant that the existential truths available through receiving knowledge have become suppressed. We are immersed in and surrounded by vast amounts of information, but often a lot doesn't matter.

To say we are in such an historical moment is, of course, an interpretation. But it's an interpretation put forward by a range of modern thinkers and artists. In the middle of the twentieth century, for example, William Carlos Williams wrote, "It is difficult / to get the news from poems / yet men die miserably every day / for lack / of what is found there."[4] Women too, would be the updated language. Further, you could update Williams's venues by adding, say, streaming TV shows and immersive exhibitions using new technologies. But the point would be the same: there is a kind

---

4. Williams, *Pictures from Breughel*, 161.

Chapter Two: On Knowing

of knowing in which something is at stake. What's at stake is *meaning*, and it can bear hard on our life and death as human subjects.

The two kinds of knowledge turn up in recent documentaries covering the Apollo space program. In 2019, renewed attention to this era was prompted by the 50th anniversary of the first manned Moon landing. Looking back to the 1960s, we can see how remarkable advances in technology and engineering enabled those first excursions beyond earth. Also striking, however, are the remarks made by some of the astronauts who first viewed the earth from space, remarks that signal a subtle shift in awareness found amid the technological feats. The utter artificiality of human national boundaries is part of what they saw. The recurrent existential question—*why is there something instead of nothing?*—seemed to loom as well. Above all, it was the recognition of the astonishing beauty and fragility of our living planet viewed against the infinite backdrop of black space that signaled the stirring of a different sort of cognizance. It's clear that innovative technological knowledge will be badly needed in grasping and facing the scope of our planet's imminent ecological catastrophe. But another kind of knowledge will figure no less into the quality and meaning of our presumed survival.

Receiving knowledge and controlling knowledge can arrive at a primary truth from different angles. For example, in a breakthrough study, *The Worm at the Core: On the Role of Death in Human Life*, Sheldon Solomon, Jeff Greenberg, and Tom Pyszczynski, use scientific analyses of the brain to explain how "the development of the neocortex spawned symbolic thought and self-awareness" in humans. This brain capacity, they note, enabled our species "to reflect on the past and anticipate the future." Thereby, we gained—or got stuck with—"knowledge of our mortality."[5]

In a surprising side note, these authors mention that our species' awareness of our mortality squares with "the biblical

---

5. Solomon et al., *Worm at the Core*, 214.

standpoint." They allude to a well-known myth in Genesis (2:15—3:24); the "fall of man" story tells how "the knowledge Adam and Eve gained by partaking of the apple made them mortal."[6] This biblical reference in a work of social science is surprising, because science, if and when it has any reason to look at sacred narratives, tends to treat them as sources of erroneous information. For instance, a fact-driven examination of Genesis might determine that, given the flora and fauna in the ancient eastern Mediterranean basin, the forbidden fruit was probably a pomegranate, not an apple. Interesting enough, but this would miss the point concerning mortality.

The authors of *The Worm at the Core* recount how they developed objective experiments to examine the implications of the fact that we are animals who know we are going to die. In a program of research conducted over three decades, they have uncovered psychological mechanisms involved in the repression of our fear of death. Under the auspices of Terror Management Theory, they have shown how cultures serve to protect us from mortality salience, while fostering our worldview defenses.

The empirical observations that verify Terror Management Theory are revealing, yet our fear of death isn't really subject to "management." Controlling knowledge can demystify the role of death anxiety in our lives, and further, look towards education and planning to assuage the problem by heightening our awareness. But the irrevocable side of our existential predicament comes into sharper focus via receiving knowledge. Literary works, for example, can depict character development and reenact complex drives that underlie the surface of normal life. This is not to downplay the aesthetic pleasure that goes with reading, or to suggest this is what all literature is up to. Yet even a gothic novel like Mary Shelley's *Frankenstein*, fanciful entertainment at one level, shows readers, first and foremost, a figure motivated by the longing for immortality. And for sheer poignancy in rendering the human flight from mortality, there is no story in world literature quite like Leo Tolstoy's *The Death of Ivan Ilyich*, an out-and-out case study in the

---

6. Solomon et al., *Worm at the Core*, 214.

Chapter Two: On Knowing

contours and labyrinths of everyday death denial. I will spotlight literary works in a later chapter.

Fiction can provide receiving knowledge, first, by creating an imaginative world that we enter, and then skewing or turning at an angle our re-entry back into the customary world. With this change in our angle of vision, assumptions held dear can now seem up for grabs. As Northrop Frye puts it, "The constructs of the imagination tell us things about human life we don't get in any other way."[7]

Mythological narratives can also enlarge what we know. This claim flies in the face of the widespread view of "myth" as simply a synonym for "false." Granted, some hobbyists today might retain a private fascination with the charm of mythic tales, but critical analysis has undermined the sacred cosmos to which myths once referred by exposing their hidden configurations of desire and power.[8] The idea of a sacred cosmos has been relegated to an infantile stage of human development.

This relegation depends on literalism. In other words, if you want to debunk a myth—say, one of the origin stories which can be found all over the planet—take its metaphors as misinformation first of all. Do not be distracted by its narrative framework or by the multiple meanings of its images and symbols. If you find its references to the sacred and to ultimate questions of living and death primitive, remember that an objective analysis need not focus on such concerns.

In opposition to literalism, however, different strains of modern thought have taken alternative approaches to understanding meaning in myth. For example, Mircea Eliade claims that *mythos* is not "a stage in the history of consciousness but a content in the structure of consciousness."[9] From this angle, humans are fully ra-

---

7. Frye, *Educated Imagination*, 53.

8. Dorrien, *In a Post-Hegelian Spirit*, 5–6.

9. Eliade, *Quest*, i. John Dominic Crossan is at pains to point out the limits of a one-dimensional approach to myth when he says, "My point is not that those ancient people told literal stories and that we are smart enough to take them symbolically, but that they told them symbolically and we are now dumb enough to take them literally. They knew what they were doing; we don't." See Crossan, *Who Is Jesus*, 79.

tional only on the basis of, and interdependence with, nonrational factors—the unconscious, for example.[10] The archetypal motions of the psyche, alive and well under the incessant innovation of modern culture, still seek connection to the ground and meaning of life. Myths once mediated this task; they unveiled the hidden wholeness of reality for particular communities, albeit through tales set in each community's concrete world of appearances. In short, myth once played a *religious* role in culture—if, that is, religion is understood, not as "belief in God," but as *religio* in the original Latin sense: *to connect* or *to bind back*. Myths might include tales of dark powers and disclose the destructive side of human nature—what William Butler Yeats called "the fury and the mire of human veins"[11]—but they also provided communities with an ameliorating sense of participation in ultimate mystery. Myths also served as guides for successful passage through the stages of life. This is evident in multiple stories of the journey of the hero found in mythologies around the world, as shown in Joseph Campbell's classic study, *The Hero with a Thousand Faces*.[12]

Myths yield receiving knowledge. Like literature and other cultural creations, they work through symbolic language. In other words, just as numbers are essential to controlling knowledge, symbols are basic to receiving knowledge. In the domain of human culture, symbols can operate differently from signs. Signs and symbols are similar in that both have referents, that is, they consist of signifiers (the physical things themselves) and signifieds (what the things mean). But where signs can be replaced by other signs, symbols cannot be substituted in the same way. For example, a red traffic light—a sign—means stop, but if enough people agreed on it, purple could be used instead. The situation is different with

---

10. Tillich, *World Situation*, 13.
11. Yeats, "Byzantium," 132–33.
12. Campbell, *Hero with a Thousand Faces*. Campbell called symbolic and metaphoric references to transcendent reality "being statements." In *Myths to Live By*, Campbell writes, "The first and most important effect of a living mythological symbol is to waken and give guidance to the energies of life" (88).

CHAPTER TWO: ON KNOWING

symbols, however, because, strange to say, symbols *participate* in the reality to which they point.[13]

One way to understand this participation factor is in terms of national flags. I grew up in Canada where the red maple leaf flag, chosen in the 1960s, has the character of a sign more than of a symbol. Many Canadians are now proud of this flag, but if I stood on a street corner in Canada and burned the flag, passersby might show a range of reactions, but responses would probably not turn violent. On the other hand, if one stood on a street corner in many areas of the US and burned an American flag (not recommended), threatening reactions might well ensue. This is because the American flag, with a great deal more history and conflict behind it, is for many Americans more of a symbol than a sign. On the whole, Americans experience their flag as intrinsic to the reality of their nation.

The ontological side of symbols—the feature that makes their signifiers participatory rather than arbitrary—can be seen especially in terms of religious representations, such as the star of David (in the Jewish tradition), the crescent (in the Islamic tradition), and the cross (in the Christian tradition). If some committee wanted to replace one of these symbols with something else—say, a new icon invented as part of an upbeat marketing strategy—the attempt would fail. It wouldn't work because persons within these traditions experience their symbols as inextricably interwoven with the meaning expressed in their sacred narratives.

Words can function as both signs and symbols, depending on the context of their usage. When words are used to convey information, they function largely as signs. They can provide and transmit controlling knowledge through their power of *denotation*. By contrast, it's the *connotative* capacity of words that comes more into play in the case of receiving knowledge. When used in this

---

13. Samuel Taylor Coleridge formulates this view of symbols in *The Statesman's Manual*. He notes that the symbol "always partakes of the reality which it renders intelligible; and while it enunciates the whole, abides itself as a living part in that unity of which it is the representative." Quoted in Franke, *Secular Scriptures*, 144.

semantic context, the figurative dimension of symbolic language has the potential to communicate meaning-laden experience. Immersion in creative language can be uncanny. Writers of both poetry and fiction report moments of surprising reversal when it feels as if language itself were speaking. Virginia Woolf, Rilke, Dante—many writers could be cited in this regard. Consider, for instance, the twentieth-century novelist William Faulkner. Over the course of his career, Faulkner wrote numerous novels and short stories that culminated in his winning of the Nobel prize for literature in 1949. On occasion, though, he would acknowledge to friends and students with some amazement, "I don't know where it came from."[14] Noting his lack of formal education, as well as the early absence of any circle of critical support, he came to regard the creative side of his life as a gift: "something worth saying knew better than I did how it needed to be said."[15]

The sense of an encounter with something larger and other than ourselves is a distinguishing feature of receiving knowledge. It turns up in a host of statements by visual artists as well. For example, the painter Paul Klee spoke of drawing and painting as a kind of "play," yet he found in this play the threshold to "an unknowing game with ultimate things."[16] Like Wassily Kandinsky, the author of *Concerning the Spiritual in Art* (2012), Klee drew imaginatively upon a depth dimension of life that outstrips our ability to control it. And because this depth is not entirely subject to human manipulation, perhaps it is also best left unnamed. Maybe it can only be alluded to in camouflaged terms, as Pablo Picasso noted late in his life. He recognized, on the one hand, that there is "something sacred" in experiencing a powerful work of art. Yet he also realized the word "sacred" is easily misconstrued. According to Picasso, "We ought to be able to say that word, or something like it, but people would take it the wrong way, and give it a meaning it hasn't got. We ought to be able to say that such and such a painting

---

14. Faulkner, *Selected Letters*, 348.

15. Quoted in Dowling, *William Faulkner*, 15.

16. Paul Klee, "Schöpferische Konfession," quoted in Martin, *Art and the Religious Experience*, 152.

Chapter Two: On Knowing

is as it is, with its capacity for power, because it is 'touched by God.' But people would put a wrong interpretation on it. And yet it's the nearest we can get to the truth."[17] Picasso knew he could not connect creative inspiration to "God" because the word had atrophied. Fundamentalists had co-opted the term to serve purely moralizing and otherworldly ends. Shorn of the incalculable, "God" had come to designate an omniscient bully operating by fiat from above. It's the God whom cosmonaut Yuri Gagarin, the first man in space, was happy to report is not there.

To summarize: art, myth, symbol, and literary works are best understood in relation to receiving knowledge. To repeat a point made at the beginning of this chapter, this is not to say that receiving knowledge is better than controlling knowledge. Instead, it is to show how it is different. It's the difference I will be drawing upon in the following chapters in order to trace out the terms of an apophatic theology. In short, such theology has an epistemological basis. It is not dependent for its currency on scientists, such as Einstein, saying a few positive things about "mystery."[18] Nor does a focus on receiving knowledge imply disparagement of controlling knowledge. Controlling knowledge is indispensable. It keeps us alive. Mathematical modelling is better than reading entrails. But the dominance of the lifeworld by controlling knowledge today means that everything in our *habitus* gets turned into an object of calculation and control. Under the conditions of global capitalism, every facet of our lives is turned over to uses of profit and action. Mindfulness becomes corporatized. Art turns into a portfolio

---

17. Picasso, *Picasso Says*, 32.

18. The battle to enlist Einstein on one side or the other in the religion vs. anti-religion debate is ongoing. On the pro-religion side, the following remark is often cited: "The most beautiful thing we can experience is the mysterious. It is the source of all true art and science. He to whom the emotion is a stranger, who can no longer pause to wonder and stand wrapped in awe, is as good as dead—his eyes are closed. The insight into the mystery of life, coupled though it be with fear, has also given rise to religion." See Einstein, *Living Philosophies*, 6.

option, a decorative pastime, or an edgy means for enhancing the shopping experience of the "personalized" masses.

In closing, the life of Charles Darwin can provide a momentary illustration of the need for different kinds of knowledge. Before publishing *The Origin of the Species* in 1859, Darwin labored for many years to establish evidence that human beings are the product of evolution. The upshot of his great discovery is that we share with all other life forms a basic biological predisposition towards survival in the service of reproduction. We got here through the combined effects of random mutation and natural selection over millions of years. That we descended, first, from tiny animals scurrying nocturnally among the dinosaurs and then from the same proto-ape as the chimpanzee is a permanent affront to all those who want to deny or escape the animality and implicit mortality of the human body, whether that be through the after-life ideologies of fundamentalists or the fantasies of technologists who hope to upload our brains onto hard drives.[19]

Late in life, Darwin spoke of the personal costs of gathering the evidence and absorbing all the information required to verify his contributions to our knowledge of evolution. In a letter to a friend, he mentions his regret at losing, in the process, his joy in reading poetry. He says he wishes he had continued to read poetry and listen to music "at least once every week." He writes, "My mind seems to have become a machine for grinding general laws out of large collections of facts." He goes on to call "the loss of these tastes [for art] . . . a loss of happiness."[20] It's a remark that could be dismissed as a throwaway elderly complaint. But it might also be taken as a testimonial of sorts: we need to look outwardly to expanding horizons to discover new facts, but also inwardly to moments of re-enchantment that show us another way to know.

---

19. See Kurzweil, *Singularity Is Near*, 206.
20. Darwin, *Autobiography of Charles Darwin*, 26.

Chapter Three: A Crack in Everything

Enjoy the bright, keep it turned up perpetually if you can, but be honest and don't deny the black. —Herman Melville[1]

A world order that commits planetary suicide in the search for profit while driving the majority of human beings into despair and poverty is a killing/producing machine without spiritual center. —Joel Kovel[2]

AT ONE LEVEL, WE are digestive tracts walking around on two legs. We have cavities at one end and hemorrhoids at the other, and we're just trying to eat, have sex, make friends, and not die. At a more exalted level, our animal brains know we are transitory. We are finite, and that means, by implication at least, we can imagine and ponder the infinite, also known as the eternal.

There is an incongruity between our limitations as biodegradable animals and our designs on life. This incongruity is a problem. It is deep-seated, and it can be described, bridged, colored, formulated, and negotiated in multiple ways—as many ways, perhaps, as there are religions. For it is religion, the depth-dimension of human culture, that, in one way or another, homes in on and addresses our problematic disconnect. Adding to the difficulty is that the effects of the disconnect catch religion in their wake.

1. Melville, "Encantadas," 104.
2. Kovel, *History and Spirit*, 12.

Next to Nothing

Human existence is shot through with splits and flaws. Things go inexhaustibly awry. Patterns of distortion may be minor yet seem impossible to overcome. Stated as a "law" or in epigrammatic form, you might say with Murphy, if it can go wrong it will go wrong, noting with chagrin, it often does so at the worst possible time. On a personal scale, we discern fault lines in our ordinary lives. On an historical scale, we know there is something deeply amiss in ongoing afflictions, such as scarcity and atrocity. We rightly fight against the social, political, and economic conditions that sustain injustice, instead of falling for the ideological trick that these conditions are natural or "God's plan." Yet progress in this fight is often followed by disappointment when struggles for justice lead only to temporary change. There are moments when any activist might wonder if John Calvin was on to something when he called the human heart "a perpetual factory of idols."[3] What lasting good can come if that is so? Even the moral philosopher Immanuel Kant, while untiring in his formulations of human dignity, felt compelled to say, "From the crooked timber of humanity no straight thing was ever made."[4] You can hear expressions of our rudimentary predicament in many areas of culture, and sometimes intimated with fine style. In music, for example, the lamentations conventional to blues lyrics are a case in point. And while driving to the dentist the other day, on the car radio, I'm sure I heard Bob Dylan sing, "Everything Is Broken."[5]

Again, the history of human cultures shows a panorama of ways to define and flesh out the dislocating factor in human life. In what follows I will touch on three ways of naming the prime flaw: *hubris* in the ancient Greek world, *dukkha* in the Buddhist path of enlightenment, and *sin* in the Judeo-Christian tradition. This will not be a systematic inquiry into these terms. Rather, they will be treated as providing a broad access point for apophatic theology. Such a perspective remains open to learning from different takes on the fissures in our lives. It is an approach that can lead

---

3. Calvin, *Institutes of the Christian Religion* (1559), 108.
4. Kant, "Idea for a Universal History," Sixth Thesis.
5. Dylan, "Everything Is Broken," *Oh Mercy*, 1989.

Chapter Three: A Crack in Everything

to ontological understanding of the human predicament, which is the starting point for finding theological meaning today.

※

For the ancient Greeks, the world would be a beautiful and magnificently ordered place—if it were left unperturbed. But things can go wrong, and disaster unfolds in patterns. In its pristine, essential arrangement, everything in the Greek cosmos was endowed with a proper share of being, a territory, as it were. This share, or *moira*, suffused every animate and inanimate object, every individual, every city-state, and every god. A principle of justice—*dike*—determined where everything properly fit in the overarching scheme of things. There was nothing egalitarian about this arrangement. For example, it went without saying that an aristocrat had immense *moira* in comparison to commoners. Even the gods figured into the ordering, which meant that conflicts could break out when the territorial reach of one god, Poseidon the sea god, for instance, was intruded upon by, say, Hades, whose proper *moira* was the underworld.

All would be well within this cosmos if every entity were to occupy its own *moira*, observe the limits set by *dike*, and not overlap or trespass upon the *moira* of another.[6] But these limits are not observed, as depicted repeatedly in Greek literature. Perhaps the most famous usurpation of proper boundaries is the abduction of Helen by Paris, the event underlying Homer's epics, *The Iliad* and *The Odyssey*.

For the Greeks, usurpation of proper limits is an act of *hubris*. In modern usage this term signifies overweening pride, with the implication that one has chosen to take this arrogant stance. But the Greeks did not view *hubris* as rooted in free decision. Encroaching upon the *moira* of another could arise out of ignorance of circumstances and consequences. Oedipus, for example, "did not know it was his father he murdered, his mother he married."[7]

---

6. For this summary of the ancient Greek world view, I am indebted to Hesla, "Greek and Christian Tragedy."

7. Hesla, "Greek and Christian Tragedy," 75.

It could also occur under delusion or through the frenzy sent by a god. Actions could stem from in-born character flaws, over which mortals have no control. Exceptional mortals were bound to find out their fateful limits and be thrown into shame, but not as culpable persons in a struggle between good and evil.

In the fifth century, Sophocles, Aeschylus, and Euripides wrote plays that reenact the calamitous suffering wrought by *hubris*. But the plots of these tragedies also integrate vital moments of recognition. In a recognition scene, as the terrible truth dawns on the protagonist, *sophia*, or wisdom acquired from suffering, also comes into view. For the audience, identification with the figures on stage could have a purging effect. According to Aristotle, viewers' imaginative witness of these stories could bring the catharsis of pity and fear, and thereby give meaning to suffering.[8]

We can read ancient Greek stories today only through a different interpretative lens. Yet we can still glean the basic lesson: our limited knowledge is part and parcel of human finitude. We can recognize that tragic blindness leads to a stripping away of vanity and pretensions to reveal essential truths of existence. The mythological tale of Icarus might serve as an example. Icarus, the son of the master craftsman Daedalus, sought to escape Crete with his father after Daedalus performed an engineering feat by constructing wings from feathers and wax. Despite the warning not to fly too low or too high, Icarus plunged into the sea and drowned after his wings melted when he ascended too close to the sun.

At one level, this ancient narrative turns on an act of encroachment of the *moira* of the gods. It was *hubris* to seize their power of flight. From our standpoint today, though, the story of Icarus might serve as a cautionary tale of a different sort. In the face of modern forms of ignorance, it could be taken as a warning about the suffering that follows from technological *hubris*. I am thinking here of massive environmental destruction, which is increasingly on display in our own time. The strife and ecological damage resulting from the oblivious pursuit of profit—the BP oil rig disaster is an example—can be traced to arrogant indifference

---

8. Aristotle, *Poetics*, chs. 9, 24, and 25.

CHAPTER THREE: A CRACK IN EVERYTHING

to environmental safety. That the entire planet is now at risk from global warming is a measure of the cost of overconfidence in technological prowess and the willful blindness that underwrites it.

To call our present-day blindness "willful" is to point up the altered context of our modern take on what goes wrong in life. In contrast to the ancient Greeks, we tend to assume that choice and contingency are involved. History is not locked endlessly into cycles. Things don't have to happen a certain way. To return to Greece, for example, we might wonder why the ancient Athenians, upon their delivery from the threat of Xerxes and Persian rule, chose to become oppressors themselves. I am thinking here of events that followed the decisive battle of Salamis (480 BCE), when the Persians, who had threatened to engulf Greece, were turned back. The Persian retreat from Europe was followed by a Greek counter-offensive and the liberation of the Greeks of the islands and Asia Minor coasts. But Athens then became an imperialist power itself. Lacking the collective wisdom to recognize its limits, Athenians now subdued and exploited the freed territories. Golden Age Athens proceeded to build its prosperity on this hegemonic control. The beauty and glory of Athens, not to mention its famous experiment with select male democracy, were extolled by Pericles in his famous funeral oration (431 BCE). *Hubris* resounds.[9] From an historical vantage point, it is not surprising that the Peloponnesian War soon followed. The war lasted for two decades and led to Athens' tragic demise. As recounted by the historian Thucydides, the Spartan-backed Thirty Tyrants finally took over the city-state, ruled by terror, and put an end to the greatness of Athens.[10]

The liability of things to go wrong in life finds a different explanation when we turn from the West to the East, in particular to the world view of Buddhism. For unlike the Ancient Greeks,

---

9. Pericles, "Funeral Oration," 111–17.
10. Thucydides, *History of the Peloponnesian War*.

Buddhism holds that ignorance can be overcome, albeit through a distinctive process of enlightenment. The good news is that we need not remain trapped in ignorance; we can come to know our true nature. Perhaps that is why in modern times, among world religions, Buddhism tends to be viewed more positively than others. It also helps that Buddhism is not theistic, since the modern world has largely dispensed with belief in God.

Buddhism began in India in the fifth century BCE (Before the Common Era) and spread to many lands. With its entry into other regions, such as China, Japan, Southeast Asia, Tibet, and more recently, North America, Buddhism has undergone multiple adaptations. I will not be rehearsing those complex developments here, nor tracing out major schools and traditions. Suffice it to say, the figure of the Buddha is central in each rendition, as are the man's teachings, which begin with the Four Noble Truths.

The first of these truths is that life is *dukkha*, or suffering. This truth is incontrovertible, yet there are nuances to note. Broadly speaking, *dukkha* is the pain that coincides with being human. The trouble with translating *dukkha* as "suffering" is that it implies we live in constant anguish. But *dukkha* is "not simply pain or distress." As one commentary notes, it is also "a host of petty, everyday annoyances."[11] It's the dislocation permeating our lives, from minor aggravation to harsh adversity. As a traditional Buddhist analogy depicts it, *dukkha* is like the wheel of a cart where the hole holding the axle is off-center.[12] The constraint in our lives is akin to the friction of a bad axle, and the grind begins at birth.

Dukkha arises from the constant craving that characterizes our lives. It is our nature to attach ourselves to what we believe will make us happy. Our ideas of what brings happiness may run the gamut from grandiose delusions of success, fame, or wealth to fantasies of immersion in sheltered normality. In any case, what

---

11. Taylor et al, *Religion and the Human Image*, 33.
12. Smith, *World's Religions*, 101. As Huston Smith puts it, "Life (in the condition it has got itself into) is dislocated. Something has gone wrong. It is out of joint. As its pivot is not true, friction (interpersonal conflict) is excessive, movement (creativity) is blocked, and it hurts."

Chapter Three: A Crack in Everything

we desire seldom seems fully to suffice, for to gain what we think we want is also to grow anxious about losing it. Deep down, we sense that our control of life, let alone our protection from threats such as sickness and decrepitude, is temporary. We know that our very lives are fleeting, but we repress this awareness. Repression, in turn, generates new means for managing our sense of dissatisfaction and lack. In short, we compensate by building character armor, that is to say, a sense of self that can shield us from the human condition. This illusory self draws self-esteem through identification with groups. Through transference, we identify with belief systems, charismatic leaders, nations, world views, and ways of life that provide a cocoon of belonging. Institutions and organizations require our participation in the illusion, and we play the game because it means survival and self-preservation. According to Buddhist philosopher David Loy, even as adults we join "the general amnesia where by each of us pretends to be an autonomous person and learns how to play the social game of constantly reassuring each other that, yes, you are a person just like me, and I'm okay, you're okay."[13]

We can get by in the state of delusion, but to put an end to *dukkha* we must address our underlying craving. We may be prompted in this direction when we come to see the endlessness of desire. Or we may realize that our attachments are ultimately empty. A further prompt may be the lingering intuition that "there is something wrong with me."[14] To perceive as much is to draw near to the Buddha's most startling teaching, namely, that there is no such thing as the self. This is the Buddhist doctrine of *anātman*, or "no self." In other words, the personal identity in which we have invested so much is really a mental fabrication. We cling to this fabrication because to let go of it would turn the logic of our world upside down. It would be devastating because our self-centeredness is performing the essential work in our everyday lives of smoothing over our groundlessness. To lose the conviction that

---

13. Loy, *Lack and Transcendence*, 31.
14. Loy, *Lack and Transcendence*, 31.

we are special selves with transcendental souls is to come face to face with our nothingness and the terror of death that goes with it.

There is a way out of this quandary, but patient discipline is required. As a constructed thing, the self can be de-constructed, yet relinquishment of the fetters of the false self and the ego's belief that it is separate demand training and commitment. The Buddhist Eightfold Path includes practices that provide a course of treatment and a path to enlightenment. For example, sitting meditation (*zazen*) is a technique that can lead to transformation. This works in part through acceptance of passing desires and fears, a process that makes them lose their power. With the cessation of compulsive patterns of desire and with freedom from constant dissatisfaction comes tremendous release and awakening. Dismantling the dualism of life and death overcomes the anxiety of impermanence. As Loy puts it, "When the sense of lack at my core transforms into an openness no longer defensive, the 'I' changes from a wound that flees itself to become the *now* that can never be lost."[15]

✥

The world view of the ancient Greeks and Buddhism proffer different ideas of why things go wrong in life. The Judeo-Christian notion of sin can be understood as another way to construe why the world is profoundly out of joint. If the Greek notion of *hubris* comes down to trespassing, and the Buddhist doctrine of *dukkha* accentuates lack, the word that best captures the meaning of sin is its etymological root: *asunder*. Sin is the condition of splitting apart. It's a name for the state of separation in the relation between human beings and the sacred ground of life—at least, that's what it signifies before literalists get hold of it.

The ancient Hebrews used a story to depict this state of separation. Set in the garden of Eden, the narrative in Genesis 2–3 revolves around four characters: Adam, Eve, a cunning serpent, and God, who likes to stroll in this idyllic abode while taking in the cool, evening breeze (Gen 3:8). The meanings that develop are

---

15. Loy, *Lack and Transcendence*, 77.

Chapter Three: A Crack in Everything

manifold and the action is archetypal. The decisive event occurs when the primordial domestic couple eats the fruit of "the tree of the knowledge of good and evil." This prohibited act "opens their eyes," but also leads to their banishment into exile outside the garden.

At one level, perhaps this myth expresses awareness of a shift from primordial harmony to discord. Above all, it captures the human predicament of being tossed into existence, the experience of birth, in other words, as a transition from dreaming innocence to the conditions of mortality. The story also tells how humans desire to be more than ephemeral creatures, but then meet the limits of finitude head on. The knowledge of good and evil gained brings awareness of the ethical consequences of free choice. As Richard Rohr describes this transition, "When knowledge comes, the whole world is turned upside down. The meaning of things begins to emerge. And more importantly, the relations between things are seen for the first time. Questions are asked and answers are sought. A strange restlessness comes over the human spirit and the enormity of error moves over the horizon like a vast shadow. Struggle emerges as the way of life. An appetite is awakened that can never be satisfied...."[16]

Again, this story depicts our condition of estrangement, not as a logical development, but as a wrenching, nonrational transition. It reenacts what modern existentialists have called the "thrownness" of life, a quality of experience felt in each and every passing moment. Differently stated, the story of Adam and Eve in Genesis 2–3 is not about an event that happened once upon a time, but a parable about our ongoing common destiny, a destiny that is fraught with hazard because it interconnects freedom and death. As theologian Dorothee Sölle summarizes it, "According to the Jewish-Christian tradition, human beings are always understood in terms of freedom. And freedom means being capable of evil."[17]

---

16. Rohr, "From Innocence to Knowledge," 2.

17. Sölle, *Thinking About God*, 44. This point is also made by Paul Kahn: "Only the free actor brings evil into the world. Just as evil is related to freedom, it is also related to death." See *Out of Eden*, 13.

The Genesis story comes loaded with cultural baggage and misconceptions. For example, the story is known to us today as "the fall of man," yet there's no word that means "fall" in the Hebrew tradition. Genesis may be an imaginative depiction of the human situation, but that has not deterred biblical literalists from treating it as an historical event. The English name Adam is a transliteration of the Hebrew word *adam*, the generic term for humankind, but that has not stopped literalists from regarding Adam as an actual guy. In the story, even though God makes the first human figure out of clay, thus showing the bond between Adam and the earth, that has not hindered fundamentalists from propounding otherworldly doctrines based on the dualism of body and soul. Finally, many astute readers have noted that, far from being weaker and more gullible than the man, the woman in Genesis 2–3 seems to be the sharper knife in the drawer and the more venturesome member of the original pair. After all, the man just passively eats what is handed to him. And yet, that has seldom prevented haters of women throughout Western history from condemning Eve for "original sin," a judgment that has repeatedly served to justify the subordination of women.[18]

Today we find the word "sin" distorted on multiple fronts. Instead of referring to the alienation inherent in the human predicament, it has come to mean, for some, simply untoward behavior, or the failure to meet the standards set by a list of do's and don't's. For others, the word has become one of the most radioactive and homophobic terms in the language of religion—as well as the favorite cudgel of religious authoritarians. Highly placed legalistic leaders in particular like to speak of "sins" and "sinners," instead of the root notion of sin because the stigmas of guilt and penance that accrue around these words help to gin up the obedience that facilitates ideological manipulation and social control.

The fact that a heavily charged word like "sin" can become so distorted may be seen as an instance of the very condition that "sin" points to in the first place. That is, the sundering and splitting

---

18. This point is made by Hodgson, *Winds of the Spirit*, 214.

Chapter Three: A Crack in Everything

that mark the human condition may occur in and through religion itself. Examples abound. A few cases are noted below.

For one, consider Psalm 139 found in the Hebrew Bible, or what Christians call the Old Testament. This is one of the world's great religious poems and it has often been set to music. Addressing YHWH through the metaphor of God as person, it uses several rhetorical formulations, including questions, to contend that YHWH is not your average territorial deity. But where, say, Psalm 24 states that "the earth is the Lord's"—news to ancient empires and to multi-national corporations today—Psalm 139 finds God to be everywhere:

> Where can I go from your spirit?
> Or where can I flee from your presence?
> If I ascend to heaven, you are there;
> If I make my bed in Sheol, you are there.

In early Hebraic thought, *Sheol*, the habitation of the dead, was not presumed to be anywhere God would go, so this assertion marks a radical utterance of faith. It combines with other recognitions of God's surprising presence. For instance, the speaker realizes that God resides in the recesses of the human self:

> O Lord, you have searched me and known me.
> You know when I sit down and when I rise up;
> you discern my thoughts from far away.
> You search out my path and my lying down
> and are acquainted with all my ways.
> Even before a word is on my tongue,
> O Lord, you know it completely.

At this juncture, the speaker is gripped by the idea that God is closer to us than we are to ourselves. The awareness that God is intimate with one's deepest thoughts, or what today we would call the subconscious, is unsettling in part, but it also builds into new personal affirmation. For to be comprehended in one's depth is also to have a place in the majestic and mysterious order of life.

Next to Nothing

There is a mood of thankfulness running through Psalm 139, and it makes this poem all the more jolting when it takes a dark turn at its climatic point:

> O that you would kill the wicked, O God,
>   and that the bloodthirsty would depart from me—
> those who speak of you maliciously
>   and lift themselves up against you for evil!
> Do I not hate those who hate you, O Lord?
>   And do I not loathe those who rise up against you?
> I hate them with perfect hatred;
>   I count them my enemies.

Here, in this startling shift towards hatred, we have a full, frontal view of "the sin of religion."[19] It's a no-brainer—surely, if God is near to me, God must hate those whom I hate. This belief is the crux of religious fanaticism wherever it appears and whenever anxious people sense how useful it could be to have an omniscient, omnipotent deity aid in slaughtering the opposition. Fortunately, the speaker seems to snap out of this murderous fantasy, and come back around to the earlier tone of veneration:

> Search me, O God, and know my heart;
>   test me and know my thoughts.
> See if there is any wicked way in me,
>   and lead me in the way everlasting.

Waking from the dream of revenge, the speaker recovers awareness of the marvel of divine presence. God may know what resides in the human heart, but to carry on in a righteous way of life, it might be best not to look too long and hard in that direction.

The destructive side of religion shows up in religious texts, but it is fully manifest in historical events. The cataclysmic wars of religion that shattered European life in the sixteenth and seventeenth centuries provide many illustrations. Viewed politically, the rise of new nation states drove the conflicts of this era, yet it's hard to understand the internecine killing sprees by Catholics

---

19. Tillich, *Shaking of the Foundations*, 49. Tillich offers an interpretation of Psalm 139 in his sermon, "Escape from God," 38–51.

CHAPTER THREE: A CRACK IN EVERYTHING

and Protestants from a purely political angle. In the Thirty Years War (1618–48), Protestants and Catholics killed each other at a rate that reduced the population of Northern Europe by one third. Drawing on historical documents, Michael Gillespie recounts one heinous episode:

> On a spring day in May 1631, Count von Tilly celebrated a mass to thank God for his conquest of Magdeburg, the chief city of the Protestant Reformation, boasting that no such victory had occurred since the destruction of Jerusalem. He was only slightly exaggerating—the cathedral in which the mass was held was one of three buildings that had not been burned to the ground. His Catholic League troops had besieged the city since November.... Once they stormed through the gates their zeal, rapacity, and greed knew no bounds. The slaughter was unstoppable. Fires were set throughout the city, children were thrown into flames, and women were raped before being butchered. Fifty-three women were beheaded in a church where they sought refuge. No one was spared—twenty-five thousand Protestants were massacred or incinerated, and of the five thousand survivors some few were noblemen held for ransom, but all the rest were women who had been carried off to the imperial camp to be raped and sold from soldier to soldier.[20]

Whatever mental acrobatics and self-deceptions teemed in the brain of Count von Tilly on the occasion of this atrocity, the fervor of his soldiers also defies comprehension. Perhaps Terror Management Theory or Stanley Milgram's studies of obedience to authority can provide clues. In any case, if the word *sin* refers to a condition in which life is "torn asunder," rather than to moral peccadilloes, it is fitting to apply that word to "the conquest of Madgeburg" and a host of other annihilations carried out in the name of religion.

The tragic reality of sin also comes to the fore when religious authorities crush freedom of thought. Two people whose work fits this bill are Giordano Bruno (1548–1600) and Marguerite Porete (1250–1300). Bruno was a Dominican friar, mathematician, and

20. Gillespie, *Theological Origins of Modernity*, 129.

philosopher who developed a cosmological theory in keeping with key Renaissance breakthroughs, including the Copernican shift to a heliocentric model of space. Leaving behind the Ptolemaic model of the heavens, which took the earth to be the stationary center of the cosmos, Bruno posited that the universe is infinite, and as such, could have no center. In this he was in keeping with other theologians (such as Nicholus of Cusa) who expanded and deepened the understanding of God through their discovery of the principle of the coincidence of opposites—the idea that in everything finite the infinite is present. In other words, the divine is not in some place alongside the world or above the world, but rather is present in everything human and natural as the power of creative unity in the universe as a whole.[21] Bruno went so far as to propose that the stars we see in the night sky are distant suns with their own planets. He even speculated, remarkably enough from our own standpoint, that these planets might foster life of their own. His insights were not anti-theological—but that was lost on the Inquisitors who arrested Bruno, declared him a heretic, and eventually had him burned at the stake. He was burned "after having an iron spike driven through his tongue because the authorities feared his eloquence at the moment of death."[22]

Marguerite Porete, a French mystic who wrote a book about divine love, was also burned at the stake. Where Bruno was a victim of the Counter-Reformation, Porete was condemned by a panel of Parisian Inquisitors in 1310. They made a special point of destroying her book, *The Mirror of Simple Souls*, before her very eyes. Nevertheless, copies of the book continued to circulate anonymously for centuries, becoming a spiritual classic in the process.[23] Along with the threat posed by her gender, not to mention the

21. See Tillich, *History of Christian Thought*, 374–75.

22. Samuelson, *Seven Ways of Looking at Pointless Suffering*, 231.

23. David Kangas notes that in 1946 Marguerite Porete was rediscovered as the author of *The Mirror of Simple Souls* following the recovery of documents in the Vatican archives. See Kangas's "Dangerous Joy." I am indebted to Kangas's study. New understanding of Porete as an indispensable figure in apophatic theology has been inspired by Sells, *Mystical Languages of Unsaying*, chs. 5 and 7.

Chapter Three: A Crack in Everything

aberrant error of writing in the vernacular, Porete's crime, for the twenty-one men who sentenced her, was to presume that she had the authority to speak about the human condition from her own experience. Rejecting the assumption that theology must confine itself to a regime of ascetic "virtues," she dared to write about the possibility and implications of unity with God through love. In developing her position, she drew on the tropes and styles of courtly love. She fashioned dramatic dialogues between allegorical characters such as Love, Virtue, and Reason in order to show different approaches to key questions.[24] While it may be difficult for modern Western persons to accept her paradoxical conclusion—namely, that humans can find the "sea of joy" intended for our lives only if we let go of our attachments to the willfulness of our egos—even hardboiled secularists might value her refusal to recant her convictions. Union with God through love is not a regular pastime today, but the need for freedom of thought is commonly grasped, and Porete remains a paragon of such freedom.[25] She continues to be an inspiration as well for those who persist in the battle against the internalized sexism of the church.

A further way in which Christianity itself has turned out to be a proving ground for its own concept of sin can be seen in the denigration of sexuality that has occurred throughout its history. This predilection stems in part from the reliance of early Christian thinkers on the philosophy of Plato. Plato's elevation of a realm of pure essences over the mundane world supported the view that the human body and its functions are corrupt, and, as such, must be controlled by higher spiritual directives. This bias led Fredrich Nietzsche to dismiss Christianity as Platonism for the masses when he launched his attack on the faith eighteen centuries after its founding.[26] But prior to the influence of Plato, certain New Testament passages had disparaged the body by associating sexuality

---

24. For excerpts from Porete's *The Mirror of Simple Souls* and analysis of her treatment of the "virtues" see Franke, *On What Cannot Be Said*, 277–84.

25. For an illuminating study of Porete's life and work, see Farley, *Thirst of God*, 33–39, 85–94, and 105–14.

26. Nietzsche, Preface to *Beyond Good and Evil*.

with impurity, with the bondage of the "flesh," and with insubordinate women. On the one hand, we find in the New Testament the Apostle Paul making a radical proclamation of equality: "There is no longer Jew or Greek; there is no longer slave or free; there is no longer male and female, for all of you are one in Christ Jesus" (Gal 3:28). But a few chapters on, we find another author, writing later in the name of Paul, uttering these reactionary words: "Let a woman learn in silence with full submission. I do not permit a woman to teach or to have authority over a man; she is to keep silent" (1 Tim 2:11–12). In short, the early church undercut the egalitarian message in the authentic Paul through later letters attributed to Paul.[27] Sexual renunciation became orthodoxy. Sexual difference was denounced. Women became identified with bodily lust and portrayed as symbols of desire and death, and thus in need of steadfast male spiritual control. Moreover, the growing cult of the virgin birth—which is not even mentioned in the earliest Gospel of Mark—sought to sanitize the birth of Jesus by removing it from any association with sexuality. Theologian Lisa Isherwood summarizes the long-range impact of these developments: "Very early on in the history of Christianity the freedom offered by the Jesus movement was lost and the bestowing of the spirit that leads to all truth was replaced by creeds, councils, and doctrines . . . enshrining male desires, demands, and powers."[28]

As an incarnational religion, how did Christianity become so estranged from the carnal human body? Since the creation story in Genesis declares creation to be good, and since the life of Jesus, as portrayed in the New Testament Gospels, shows God as present in the physical world, why did the church fathers increasingly marginalize our physical nature as they established the intellectual foundations of Christianity? Their newfound authority stemmed

---

27. The different voices and theological positions attributed to Paul in the New Testament are explained by Borg and Crossan in *The First Paul*.

28. Isherwood and Horst, *Contemporary Theological Approaches to Sexuality*, 9. In this collection of essays see also "Sexual Renunciation in Christian History and Theology" by Sara Moslener, who writes, "Throughout the history of Christianity, the practice of sexual renunciation functioned to consolidate different forms of ecclesiastical or political power" (90).

Chapter Three: A Crack in Everything

in part from the altered status of Christianity at the end of the ancient world. For the first 300 years, Christians were an oppressed minority. But after Constantine made Christianity the religion of the Roman Empire in the fourth century CE, Christians were no longer hiding in catacombs. The upshot is that Christian institutional forms increasingly adapted Roman legal systems and social norms. Condoning slavery and patronage became customary. The entrenchment of patriarchal privilege within the church dovetailed with promotion of sexual renunciation. This trend culminates in Saint Augustine, Bishop of Hippo (354–430), particularly in his signature doctrine of "original sin." Prior to his conversion to early Christianity in 386, Augustine had lived a libidinous life in pagan Carthage. But like many men who, after having extensive sexual experience themselves decide it is inappropriate for others, Augustine increasingly came to define sin in sexual terms. This was partly due to his disgust with the widespread debasement of sexuality that he saw all around him. He concluded that sin is passed down through the generations biologically, literally in semen. Everyone is thereby born into corruption. We desire to do bad things whether we know it or not. The implications of this doctrine of "original sin" have been enormous. For many people, the Christian faith comes pre-packaged with the idea that salvation is gained through sexual repression, and bundled with it, the burden of assuming one's inherent wickedness. As the Christian philosopher Paul Ricœur puts it, "The harm that has been done to souls, during the centuries of Christianity, first by the literal interpretation of the story of Adam, and then by the confusion of this myth, treated as history, with later speculations, principally Augustinian, about original sin, will never be adequately told."[29] Probably not, but you

---

29. Ricœur, *Symbolism of Evil*, 239. Many modern authors have expressed dismay, disgust, and anger over this legacy of repression and the tragic fracturing of lives in relation to sexuality. For example, Richard Holloway writes, "Sadly, Christianity has been more intent on repressing and misrepresenting sex than on helping people manage it wisely." See Holloway's *Leaving Alexandria*, 74. Contemporary Lutheran minister, Nadia Bolz-Weber, writes, "I propose a sexual reformation for those who have been hurt. I also propose it for those who have done the hurting, for those who doubt my authority and

might try to tell people that tearing the embodied human self from its joyful erotic roots is a horrific instance of what sin meant in the first place.

❧

We have been looking at the ways different traditions explain how things go wrong in life by using the examples of the Greek world view and the Buddhist and Christian religions. In the case of Christianity, we also looked at how its take on what's tragically wrong with life applies no less to the career of religion itself.[30] Of course, many other religions and world views could be looked at from this comparative perspective. We could include Gnosticism, for example, which envisions the cosmos as a battle zone between dueling forces of good and evil. This view is as old as ancient Mesopotamia, where some stories depict a sinister world, a creation so full of pointless suffering only an evil god could have made it. Aspects of the Gnostic outlook turn up in contemporary pop culture, where superheroes battle it out in stories that endlessly reconfigure the conundrum of good versus evil.

Instead of cataloguing ways of explaining evil, I want to turn to some overarching insights afforded by the field of ontology. I first broached the topic of ontology in the introduction. I realize that the language of ontology, and terms such as *being* and *non-being*, can sound empty. Yet to think in ontological terms and to ask questions about the nature of being is to open doors of understanding that otherwise remain closed. For example, to understand that God, in the most precise philosophical sense, means *being itself*, and not *a separate being*, is to move beyond much hackneyed talk

---

those who are certain they know all there is to know about what God thinks of sex. It's time for us to grab some matches and haul our antiquated and harmful ideas about sex and bodies and gender into the yard. . . . And I'm not suggesting we make a few simple amendments; new wine in old skins ain't gonna cut it. I'm saying let's burn it the fuck down and start over. Because it's time." See Bolz-Weber, *Shameless*, 12–13.

30. Two authors who discuss the distorted treatment of sin as a manifestation of sin itself are Chris Hedges in *American Fascists* and Rachel Sophia Baard in *Sexism and Sin-Talk*.

Chapter Three: A Crack in Everything

about faith, especially the reduction of faith to the will to believe in unbelievable things. Granted, "being" can seem intangible, but just because the notion of being is abstract doesn't mean its reality has no bearing on our lives. Our obliviousness in this regard is nicely captured by way of analogy in an anecdote noted by David Foster Wallace: "*There are these two young fish swimming along, and they happen to meet an older fish swimming the other way, who nods at them and says, 'Morning, boys, how's the water?' And the two young fish swim on for a bit, and then eventually one of them looks over at the other and goes, 'What the hell is water?'*"[31] Our "water" can be interpreted as our immersion in being. We take our ongoing existence for granted. Perish the thought that our lives might never have been at all.

The shocks of loss—of non-being—make us see the wonder and fragility of our lives. The effects of such wake-up calls have been noted by existentialist thinkers in particular.[32] Under the aegis of modern existentialism, a range of philosophers have made the same ontological point: humans are never not a mixture of being and non-being. We are finite; we contain our end within ourselves. Beginning with Soren Kierkegaard (1813–55), these thinkers focus on our immediate and personal appropriation of our transitoriness.[33] They foreground inquiries into what it means to be authentically alive. They ask questions that arise once we become conscious that we will die. Kierkegaard, for instance, examines the role that anxiety plays in our lives, even though it is largely hidden under the surface of everyday social conformity. But he also shows that anxious awareness of death is a prerequisite to spiritual awakening. Martin Heidegger (1889–1976) emphasizes the question of being—why is there something and not

---

31. This anecdote is the linchpin in David Foster Wallace's 2005 Commencement Address at Kenyon College, "This Is Water."

32. Walsh makes this clear in *Modern Philosophical Revolution*.

33. Kierkegaard makes this point through his pseudonym Johannes Climacus in *Concluding Unscientific Postscript*. As Climacus puts it, death may be something in general for systematicians, "but for me, my dying is by no means something in general." "Suppose death," Climacus asks, "were insidious enough to come tomorrow?" (149).

nothing?—and shows that we exist as *being-in-the-world* through complex engagement with the situation into which we are thrown. Jean-Paul Sartre (1905–80) fixates on the inescapable element of freedom in individual human life and the need to be aware of our death in order to choose what is important.

Some modern philosophers forgo the terms *being* and *non-being* and speak of *becoming* instead. They underscore the point that our lives are always in process and that we experience life as constant change. To avoid the inertness of words like *being*, they combine metaphors with abstractions to bring their philosophical claims down to earth. Sartre, for example, in his eight-hundred-page opus, *Being and Nothingness*, tells us that "non-being lies coiled in the heart of being—like a worm."[34] Leaving aside the question of whether this analogy is fair to worms, the point is that non-being continuously negates being. Being, moreover, is best understood, not as something huge and stagnant in back of it all, but dialectically, as power, as the *negation of non-being's negation*. Stated another way, it is the meaning we experience when meaninglessness is overturned. Loss and affirmation make up the dynamic character of existence, the granular life we feel moment to moment as embodied finite freedom. Or as William Blake more poetically puts it, for human beings "joy and woe are woven fine."[35]

Existentialist thinking plays in a different key when religion is factored in. Religious existentialist insights are central to apophatic theology, including the apophatic work you are presently reading. To reiterate the definition offered in chapter 1, apophatic theology seeks to highlight the place of absence in our lives. From this angle, religious words such as "evil" and "demonic" find currency. These words point to the visceral experience of loss and to levels of human destruction that, in one way or another, exceed rational explanation. For example, we know that in World War II, approximately 60 million people died between 1939 and 1945. Social scientific and historical studies have shown how this war started,

---

34. Sartre, *Being and Nothingness*, 56.

35. Blake, "Auguries of Innocence," quoted in Harries, *The Beauty and the Horror*, 7.

Chapter Three: A Crack in Everything

how it developed, and why it ended. Yet statistics, concepts, and evaluations cannot corral the scope of human suffering. To watch film footage of the Nazi concentration camps or view pictures of fire-bombed Dresden is to glimpse something unspeakable that defies reasonable analysis.

The problem with the word "evil," however, is that it is readily subject to abuse. This abuse can range from the outright foolish—I am thinking here of fundamentalist Pat Robertson's claim that the 2010 earthquake in Haiti stemmed from the country's "pact with the devil"—to sophisticated cover for ideological agendas. Religious conservatives, for example, are prone to spiritualize inequality and unjust material conditions by claiming, on account of evil, that's "the way things are." You also hear the word "evil" deployed in highfalutin speeches about the sacrificial cost of attaining "the good," as if a tally of human lives could be figured into some sort of moral computation. This same "payment" mentality turns up in the religious sphere with the idea of God as an abusive father who orchestrates death as the toll for forgiveness, a prize that always comes bound up with punitive and authoritarian strings.

But while the word "evil" can be misused, dispensing with the notion altogether is problematic too. Talk of evil has been largely expunged from the discourse of modernity in its turn towards secularization. The movement behind that turn is "exclusive humanism," a movement that aims for a future in which all people can flourish.[36] For exclusive humanism, this goal can only be hindered by the archaic mentality of religion and its urges for otherworldly transcendence. Criticizing religion is thus a key to building a humane, secular world. Or as Karl Marx put it, the criticism of religion is "the premise of all criticism." This task has been carried out by modern "masters of suspicion" from several angles.[37] For example, Sigmund Freud argued that religion comes down to

---

36. Taylor, *Secular Age*, 19.

37. Marx states, "The criticism of religion is the premise of all criticism," in "Contribution to the Critique of Hegel's *Philosophy of Right*," 53. The term "hermeneutics of suspicion" is developed by Ricœur in "The Symbol Gives Rise to Thought" in Ricœur, *Symbolism of Evil*, 347–57.

unresolved childhood neurosis. Ludwig Feuerbach showed that many religious concepts are really projections—projections of powers that are human at base. In brief, uncovering the delusions and constrictions of religion paves the way for the maturation of humanity and for the modern project of rationally transforming the world. Where religion takes injustice as a given—"the poor will always be with you" is a typical refrain—concrete political action works to enact change, as is evident in the revolutionary fight to free the poor from the conditions of economic exploitation.

And yet, exclusive humanism is not without its own delusions. It conflates religion with reactionary standpoints and magical thinking. It ignores spiritual movements all over the planet that are also fighting for social justice now. (I will discuss further aspects of this struggle in chapter 4.) Exclusive humanism also skips over the question of those who are left out of a progressive future. This question does turn up, however, in modern literature. It finds expression in works by writers who are wary of the utopian bent of progressive humanism. Herman Melville's short story, "Bartleby, the Scrivener," is a case in point. On the one hand, the first-person narrator of this tale is happy to report that his "masterly management" skills have established him in a solid position within advancing civilization. At the same time, after his encounters with his destitute worker, Bartleby, he finds it hard to stop thinking about the "lost" and the fact that there is no way to redeem the meaningless suffering of "those who [have] died stifled by unrelieved calamities."[38] Framed in a different way, this issue also turns up in *The Brothers Karamazov*, by Fyodor Dostoevsky. In a dialogue between Ivan and Alyosha at the heart of the novel, Ivan refuses to ignore the reality that vast millions of people will never experience humane life in a better society. In effect, they are deemed to be "manure for someone's future harmony," as Ivan sarcastically puts it.[39] In *Notes from Underground*, Dostoevsky interrogates the limits of progressive reason as well. His nameless character, the "underground man," is a fictional creation, yet over

38. Melville, "Bartleby the Scrivener," 45.
39. Dostoevsky, *Brothers Karamazov*, 244.

Chapter Three: A Crack in Everything

the course of the novel, this figure functions as an indictment of enlightened society's failure to account for the irrational side of humans. Through the "underground man," Dostoevsky warns the modern world about the self-contradictory power of human freedom, including the freedom to lay waste to the best laid plans for human flourishing.

In summary, you can exclude religion from the modern scene, but the dark side of human freedom and the demonic implications of history return. The gap between what is and what should be reels into view, whether we understand it in terms of *hubris, dukkha, sin,* or a host of other names. We might see that gap on a global scale in the ongoing carnage of war. Or we might see it when past horrors resurface amid the wishful optimism of our consumer culture. But it is in our personal lives that the gap between what is and what should be registers most urgently. It is all too manifest to those who are in grief, in despair, in sickness, or in the throes of addiction—that is, in anyone who has ever been split apart.

The title of this chapter comes from the poem "Anthem" by Leonard Cohen. Master of paradox that he is, Cohen follows an ominous line—"There is a crack in everything"—with the promise of hope: "That's how the light gets in."[40] I want to conclude this chapter with a view to such hope, that is, the kind of hope that neither denies nor succumbs to the darkness in our lives.

For these lines from "Anthem," Cohen has drawn upon a creation story from the Kabbalist tradition of Jewish mysticism. The story begins with God's withdrawal of himself (*tzimtzum*) from a central point within himself, creating an empty space. God then emanates supernal light into the empty space. The story proceeds through several stages, including the shattering of vessels and the scattering of the light in the form of sparks. The task of humans is

---

40. Cohen, "Anthem," 373.

to recover and redeem the scattered sparks (*tukkun*).[41] As a myth, this story has affinities with the Christian interpretation of the exile of Adam and Eve as a "fortunate fall." Elaborated by John Milton in *Paradise Lost*, the outcome of this rendering is that God ultimately turns disaster into an immense good. In both the "fortunate fall" account (however unfortunately named) and in the Kabbalist myth, we wind up with a world in which humans can come to know the goodness of creation. The possibility for choosing evil is always present, for it is impossible to have both freedom and the absence of potential evil. Nevertheless, we are sojourners in a world in which we have the power to "choose life" (Deut 30:19), a place where we can come to know love, trust, joy, and genuine beauty in our lives.

We also have the power to witness and to remember. For instance, we can speak out about history's anonymous victims of violence. Instead of regarding them as fodder for human progress, the callous view that angers Ivan Karamazov, we are called upon to recall and to honor the lives of the dispossessed. As Paul Ricœur puts it, we do this in part by telling their stories. As he writes in *Time and Narrative*, "We tell stories because in the last analysis human lives need and merit being narrated." In opposition to triumphalist views of human progress, Ricœur speaks of "the necessity to save the history of the defeated and the lost. The whole history of suffering cries out for vengeance and calls for narrative."[42] We can do no other.

We also come to know the goodness of creation through the wonderful experience of healing. It can, of course, be bodily and material. Healing occurs spiritually when faith opens us to receive a power greater than ourselves, a power that turns us, transforms us, and reconciles us to ourselves and to God, where again, God is discerned as the *ground of being*, not *a being*. It can happen in moments of grace when our self-hatred falls away, and along with it, our hatred of others. Transformative healing can occur slowly

---

41. For this outline of the Lurianic Kabbalah creation myth I am indebted to Biale and Miles, *Norton Anthology of World Religions: Judaism*, 439.

42. Ricœur, *Time and Narrative*, 1:75.

Chapter Three: A Crack in Everything

and quietly over a lifetime. It may also arrive dramatically in moments of revelation. Such a moment is famously described by the twentieth-century monk and social activist, Thomas Merton. He writes about a flash of awareness that finds him unexpectedly in the midst of mundane concerns: "In Louisville, at the corner of Fourth and Walnut, in the center of the shopping district, I was suddenly overwhelmed with the realization that I loved all those people, that they were mine and I theirs, that we could not be alien to one another even though we were total strangers. It was like waking from a dream of separateness...."[43]

In an instance of awakening not unlike Merton's, the Czech writer and statesman, Vaclav Havel, describes a realization that comes to him, against odds, behind bleak prison walls. On a day when he is gazing over the prison fences and watchtowers, he is startled by the image of a tree silhouetted against the "endless sky." He struggles to describe the sensation that overtakes him:

> I seemed to rise above all the coordinates of my momentary existence in the world into a kind of state outside time in which all the beautiful things I have ever seen and experienced existed in a total "co-present"; I felt a sense of reconciliation, indeed of an almost gentle assent to the inevitable course of events as revealed to me now.... A profound amazement at the sovereignty of Being became a dizzy sensation of tumbling endlessly into the abyss of its mystery; an unbounded joy at being alive.... I was flooded with a sense of ultimate happiness and harmony with the world and with myself, with that moment, with all moments I could call up, and with everything invisible that lies behind it and has meaning. I would even say that I was somehow "struck by love," although I don't know precisely for whom or what.[44]

In such moments, life reunites with life. These epiphanies pass, but they alter the quality of ongoing experience by awakening us to the proximity of numinous meaning. It is meaning that is present

---

43. Merton, *Conjectures of a Guilty Bystander*, 156.
44. Havel, *Letters to Olga*, 331–32.

in the things of this world, but it also transcends the world as the hope and promise of overcoming estrangement.

The breakthroughs described by Merton and Havel may be taken as emblematic. In Cohen's terms, they are moments when "the light gets in." In ontological language, they are moments when the power of being itself is disclosed. In the language of chapter 2, they are moments when the sacred ground of being and meaning opens to us as receiving knowledge.

Yet we are bound to ask, if this sacred ground is good—if God is good—how do we account for the power of non-being? From whence comes the power of destruction in the world and in the hearts of humans? A standard religious approach is to go around this problem by declaring it an inscrutable mystery. Case closed. A standard philosophical approach is to formulate the problem as consisting of three propositions: (1) God is good, (2) God is omnipotent, and (3) there is evil in the world. Logically speaking, one of these three statements must be false, a conclusion that purportedly refutes all rational belief in God.

An alternative approach is to view the problem of the power of non-being as profoundly revelatory.[45] What is revealed is the living and dialectical nature of the divine ground of life. That is, life can be both creative and destructive, both dangerous and great, because non-being is dependent on the being it negates. In other words, being itself, the sacred ground and abyss of life, is not some vapid thing in back of it all forever identical with itself. It is not fixed beyond the world in ethereal perfection. Rather, non-being makes God a living God. In the words of a contemporary poet, "God goes, belonging to every riven thing he's made."[46] And, we might add, every riven thing includes humans with their gendered, anthropomorphic metaphors for God. Or as Paul Tillich puts it in philosophical terms in *The Courage to Be*, "If one is asked how non-being is related to being itself, one can only answer

---

45. This view is formulated by several modern theologians with an existential or an apophatic bent. For example, see Hall, *Cross in Our Context*, 88–89. Tillich makes this point in *Eternal Now*, 61.

46. Wiman, *Every Riven Thing*, 24.

Chapter Three: A Crack in Everything

metaphorically: being 'embraces' itself and non-being. Being has non-being 'within' itself as that which is eternally overcome in the process of the divine life."[47]

What I referred to in chapter 1 as apophatic theology fits with Tillich's view here. First of all, such theology begins, not with religious dogma, but with the human situation wherein we encounter loss. Secondly, its modus operandi is to give the negative its due. It does not "deny the black," to use Melville's phrase. It does not look to conclusive victories over evil or talk of divine omnipotence. It is a perspective that is fully aware of the deep void of meaninglessness in the modern world. At the same time, an apophatic theologian knows that when meaninglessness is overturned and new meaning arises, it does so fragmentarily and in ways not subject to our control. Such theology is rooted in faith, but faith that fully acknowledges doubt. It is the kind of faith that can lead us to center our lives around the experience of love and the saving power of compassion, yet without presuming that suffering has thereby been quarantined. In the words of theologian Wendy Farley, "Divine compassion is the power of redemption, realized in history within its tragic structures and in the midst of rupture. Redemption, therefore, cannot mean a final victory over historical evil. It remains fragmentary, always subject to defeat. Redemption cannot mean that radical suffering and sin are not destructive, or that their destructions are irrelevant or unreal. . . . But precisely in the depth of this destruction a power remains to resist it, to thwart it, to preserve the possibility of healing."[48]

Healing and new meaning arise out of that depth and meet us in our everyday lives as they unfold under the conditions of the historical moment. The relationship between our historical predicament and eternity is the subject of the following chapter.

---

47. Tillich, *Courage to Be*, 34.
48. Farley, *Tragic Vision and Divine Compassion*, 132.

Chapter Four: When the Light Gets In

We must breathe time as fishes breathe water. —Denise Levertov[1]

The heart has its reasons that reason does not know. —Blaise Pascal[2]

We are not like each other. . . . But in being neighbor we are all unconditionally like each other. . . . The neighbor is eternity's mark—on every human being. —Soren Kierkegaard[3]

IF YOU LISTEN TO people recall occasions when they learned something in school, they often skip times spent in classrooms. Rather, they remember unanticipated instances and things learned from passing conversations, or during random encounters when they were not expecting to be taught. This happens to students, but also to teachers, as I can attest from an occasion when I was teaching some William Blake poems in a community college classroom. One poem included the following lines: "To see a World in a Grain of Sand / And a Heaven in a wild Flower / Hold infinity in the palm of your hand / And eternity in an hour."[4]

Blake's works are relevant today because his words and images evoke compelling existential concerns otherwise precluded

1. Levertov, "Variation and Reflection," 779.
2. Pascal, *Pensées*, 118.
3. Kierkegaard, *Works of Love*, 89.
4. Blake, "Auguries of Innocence," 88.

Chapter Four: When the Light Gets In

by more basic needs that must be met to survive in our finance-dominated capitalist world. When people are just trying to get by, there is little time to ponder abstract ideas. So, at the end of my Blake class, when a student came up to my desk, I assumed I would be fielding a practical question, such as, "Is there a final exam in this course?" Instead, the student surprised me when he said, "No offense, Professor Champion, but I have to say I don't give a rat's ass about eternity." The words hung in the air for a moment, and then we both laughed. If humor stems from bringing unlike things together, it's not every day you hear "rat's ass" and "eternity" uttered in the same breath. We had to clear the room to make way for the next class, so we continued talking outside.

The student went on to make his case. He said that we are in this world for a short time and then we pass on. In his words, "We kick the bucket. We come to *nothing* in the end, so it's ridiculous to claim there's some big meaning to it all." Then came the clinching point: "Just because life is meaningless, it doesn't mean it's not worth living." I responded in accordance with my teacher training by floating a question: "Don't you think meaning is implied in the word 'worth'?" I mentioned a few Stoic philosophers whom the student might enjoy reading. I doled out some generic remark about the value of thinking about these things. But then I found myself saying, "No offense, but your *nothing* is too small." The words hung in the air for a moment, and their illogic was lost on neither of us. Afterwards I realized I had made the remark because my own experience of loss of meaning had, over time, proven to be deeper-running than every work-around I could fashion, including my own feigned nonchalance.

Which brings me to this moment in my life and to a chapter highlighting the problem of nothingness. The problem is treated here predominantly in terms of the absence of meaning and the possibility of the creation of new meaning. My overarching framework is a discussion of eternity and of how eternity can be seen to bear on our lives today. Eternity is understood throughout not as a really long time but as a qualitative dimension of each and every passing moment of our lives. That this dimension, far from inducing us to escape from this world, leads us into the struggle for social justice now is the paradoxical assertion made in this chapter's final section.

❦

Talk of eternity is suspect for many people because it smacks of religion and brings religion to the fore at a time when religion is, in my student's words, "so over." Fundamentalists think it's over because their own beliefs are not mere religion. Their beliefs are "the truth," of which they are in sole possession. It is other people who have religions, which are significant insofar as they point to rival pools of potential converts. Dogmatic secularists, on the other hand, think religion is finished because it is based on magical thinking. Science and technology now provide the knowledge we need. Secularists may have moments when they admit that not all religion is fundamentalist, but they pivot to say that nonfundamentalist religion is of no consequence today. It is of no more use now than an outdated travel guide.

Fundamentalists and anti-religionists are similar in some respects. Both camps think faith entails claims of fact—it's just that one side is sure these facts are available through confessional acts, while the other side knows the information is false. But more importantly, these positions smooth over our existential condition. Ontologically put, both sides suppress our proximity to nothingness. In different directions, both camps elide the precariousness of human life and the frailties we share beneath our character armor and our worldviews.

Fundamentalists cover up the human condition through the denial of death. They believe we are ushered into heaven or we go through a round of reincarnations that circumvent the reality of dying. Denial of death, in short, is the key to fundamentalism. In making this point, my claim is that fundamentalism is not, as many commentators would have it, social and economic at base. According to that social scientific approach, fundamentalism is primarily a reaction against the impact of neo-liberalism and global neo-colonialism. From this angle, major forms of fundamentalism

CHAPTER FOUR: WHEN THE LIGHT GETS IN

today—in Christianity, in Islam, and in Hinduism—are treated as resistance movements that have harnessed religion as a means for conveying class and racial grievances. Or fundamentalism is explained as a mobilizing tool in the fight against colonized knowledge and Western-led expansion. Or it's analyzed as a vehicle for motivating extreme nationalist militias. But as Sathianathan Clarke points out in *Competing Fundamentalisms*, while economic and political factors certainly play a role in the rise of religious fundamentalism, it is a mistake to view all religion as a by-product of such forces.[5]

We can see that something besides economics is at work when we take note of the expressions and visions that fuel the global upsurge of fundamentalism today. For "crusading disciples" in Christianity, "mullah militants" in Islam, and "kshatriya sanyasis" in Hinduism—a surprising development given Hinduism's long-time restriction to Mother India—the entire world must fall into line.[6] First and foremost, the master narratives of secularism and modernity must be abolished. This desire to annul the founding stories of "others" stems from the menace posed by their presence in the world. That is, their rival utterances and representations trigger reminders of death, for they stir up implicit questions as to whether one's own prospect for immortal life is true—or, at least, as unassailable as advertised within one's group account. Alternative worldviews and ways of life threaten to undo the significance of life and to disassemble safeguards against the terror of death.

---

5. Clarke, *Competing Fundamentalisms*, 20. To a lesser extent, Clarke also discusses instances of Jewish and Buddhist terrorism.

6. As Clarke points out, "Religious fundamentalism has become much more dangerous over the last several decades as it has projected its ambitions onto a global screen" (*Competing Fundamentalisms*, 143). A common characteristic of Christian, Muslim, and Hindu fundamentalisms is that "they take as their object the establishment of a global order in which their respective Word-visions can dictate the world-ways of all humanity" (144). On the global ambitions of Hinduism—a surprising development given the Hindu religion's traditional disinterest in the world beyond India—Clarke refers to developments that have followed the Hindu Nationalist party's 2014 successes; he cites statements like those of Sai Baba: "By 2020 the entire country will be Hindu and by 2030 the entire world will be Hindu" (151).

As Richard Beck writes in *The Slavery of Death*, the person with other beliefs "threatens us to the core, attacks the very source of our self-esteem. This means that . . . the out-group member who is simply different from us doesn't have to do anything particularly threatening. His or her mere *existence* is enough to menace us."[7] Within the closed circles of fundamentalist belief systems, the perceived menace can quickly elevate killing into a veritable calling. In times of crisis, failure to grasp this eliminationist dynamic in fundamentalism can have lethal consequences for persons of good will who think fundamentalists might be interested in hearing different points of view.

The fear of death underlying fundamentalist religion surfaces when its adherents turn violent. By contrast, we less readily associate violence with those who are determined to extricate themselves from religion altogether. But while more peaceable, the "cultured despisers of religion,"[8] to use Schleiermacher's phrase, are not immune to death anxiety. In other words, the rigorously secular, like the religious, find self-esteem and assurance by adhering to the standards and convictions of like-minded persons. Moreover, there is an uplifting pride in becoming self-reliant and in gaining freedom from superstition and fears of the unknown beyond the grave. Still, among those happy to have thrown off the delusions of religion, a longing for life beyond our "mortal coil" can linger. Should wayward impulses for immortality flare up, equanimity can be restored in a number of ways. For example, we can alleviate fear of passing meaninglessly into the void by bringing children into the world. Thereby names and legacies will go on.[9] The finality of death can also be countered symbolically. Contributing to science and technology, creating works of art, erecting buildings, meeting philanthropic challenges—there are many ways to fit this

---

7. Beck, *Slavery of Death*, 41.
8. Schleiermacher, *On Religion*.
9. Science writer Brian Greene takes note of this impulse in *Until the End of Time*. Greene writes, "Some soothe the existential yearning through commitment to a family, a team, a nation—construct a religion that will outlast the individual's allotted time on earth" (5).

Chapter Four: When the Light Gets In

bill. Andy Warhol's quip that "in the future everyone in the world will be famous for fifteen minutes"[10] is a joke in part, but it's also an astute observation of the conditions for cultural heroics in a world devoted to the provisos of self-sufficient finitude.

Where fundamentalists hope to see the triumph of their beliefs, secularists assume that religion will end altogether. They adhere to the "subtraction" story of secularization in which modernity inevitably leads to the demise of the need for religion. But in dismissing religion, secularists are sometimes blind to the deep roots of their own causes. Human rights provide a telling example. Lest the cause of human rights be tainted by religion, secularists downplay the *imago Dei*, that is, the biblical conception that all human beings are created in God's own image (Gen 1:26–28). On the one hand, colonialism and white supremacist theology exploited this doctrine to justify patriarchy, empire-building, slaughter, and enslavement. On the other hand, throughout Western history, this idea has inspired many movements to fight for the freedom, moral standing, and intrinsic dignity of every human being, a stance that has included struggles against intolerant forms of religion.[11] But strict secularists, ever alert—and rightly alert—to the harmfulness of religion, frame the battle for universal human rights as a purely humanist affair. The fight for human rights begins with the eighteenth-century European Enlightenment, so the story goes.[12]

---

10. This statement by Andy Warhol appeared on a poster for Warhol's 1968 retrospective at the Moderna Museet in Stockholm, Sweden. See Gopnik, *Warhol*, 604–5.

11. For an overview of the image-of-God doctrine, see Peppiatt, *Imago Dei*. Peppiatt notes that this doctrine is "multifaceted and constantly evolving" (129). For an analysis of human rights see Joas, *Sacredness of the Person*. On the religious roots of human rights see Osborn, *Humanism and the Death of God*, 179 and 204. To claim the imago Dei can inspire struggles for justice is not to deny that it has also been used to justify untold exploitation by alleging that God ordained humans to assume godlike dominion over the rest of creation. In particular, the doctrine of discovery, backed by fifteenth-century papal bulls, provided the theological justification for European Christian capitalists to dominate lands inhabited by indigenous peoples. I will return to this issue in chapter 5.

12. For a dismissal of the connection between human rights and religion

Granted, nonauthoritarian and nonliteralist religious groups have fought for human rights in the past and are fighting for human rights around the world today, but secularists treat these developments as anomalies in the end.

Popular forms of atheism likewise omit religion from the narrative of human progress. Historical *lacunae* ensue. As Scott Samuelson notes, "Many atheists abandon belief in God like it was giving up belief in the tooth fairy and then live as unconscious parasites on the slowly dying carcass of the culture born of that god." By way of example, Samuelson points out that "our liberal democratic institutions and habits are nourished by sacred background beliefs. The concept of 'justice,' for instance, relies on the idea that there's an order of right and wrong transcending politics."[13]

NIETZSCHE AND KIERKEGAARD

Many atheists, free of the "tooth fairy" God, cite Friedrich Nietzsche as their precursor. There is a certain irony in this, however, in that Nietzsche was no friend of democratic and liberal thinking vital to modern secular society. Rather than disappearing under the impact of modernity, religion, in Nietzsche's view, continued to play a role—albeit a debasing one—in shaping history and culture. In fact, that's why many theologians today recognize the importance of Nietzsche, even if they don't agree with him that God is dead.[14] Nietzsche attacked the religious roots of culture in the

---

see Ignatieff, *Human Rights as Politics and Idolatry*, 82–88. According to Ignatieff, "There is nothing sacred about human beings, nothing entitled to worship or ultimate respect. All that can be said about human rights is that they are necessary to protect individuals from violence and abuse, and if it is asked why, the only possible answer is historical." Ignatieff expresses disdain for any religious perspective when he writes, "The religious side believes that only if humans get down on their knees can they save themselves from their own destruction; a humanist believes that they will do so only if they stand up on their own two feet."

13. Samuelson, *Seven Ways of Looking at Pointless Suffering*, 58.

14. As Samuelson puts it, "One of the reasons that many believers in God appreciate Nietzsche is that he sees clearly just how integrated religion is into

Chapter Four: When the Light Gets In

name of a greater life-giving principle. He railed against the slave mentality of religious beliefs, and he held special disdain for Christianity on account of its concern for the weak and the lowly. Yet atheists who identify with Nietzsche's heroic critique often seem unaware of his embrace of the aristocratic will to power. Do they realize that Nietzsche wanted to jettison the very idea of rights? It's one thing to act out a Nietzschean fantasy and imagine you have dispensed with religion, but quite another to see tragedy at the heart of life and, with Nietzsche, joyfully affirm life nevertheless.[15]

Superficial readings of Nietzsche by secularists reveal blind spots in secularism and show that secularists have a way of recapitulating narrow-minded religion—the kind of religion, that is, that demonizes atheists. Religious authoritarians, on the one hand, seek cognitive and behavioral control through dogma and mystification. On the other hand, secularists, are not without their own control issues.[16] When every appeal to transcendence or the divine as a source of value and meaning is dismissed in favor of materialist accounts, secularism colonizes the mystery of being. With that mystery defused, the heartfelt question *does my life matter?* gets relegated to an adolescent tick. Concern with eternal time recedes as well. *Ultimacy* is superseded by the nonstop *interesting*, the stream of information catching our attention and monopolizing our time. As Charles Taylor writes in *A Secular Age*, "We have constructed an environment in which we live a uniform, univocal secular time, which we try to measure and control to get things

---

culture" (*Seven Ways of Looking at Pointless Suffering*, 58).

15. In 1875, Nietzsche launched a scathing attack on Christianity's slave morality of compassion: "In Christianity the instincts of the subjugated and oppressed come into the foreground: it is the lowest classes which seek their salvation in it" (*Twilight of the Gods and the Anti-Christ*, 31.) In *Beyond Good and Evil*, Nietzsche argues that "among humans as among every other species of animal there is a surplus of deformed, sick, degenerating, frail, necessarily suffering individuals" and Christianity's support for such weaklings is leading to "the degeneration of the European race," 56–57. Alex Ross provides a fine overview of different approaches to Nietzsche in "Eternal Return," 34–37. Taylor offers an insightful discussion of Nietzsche in *Secular Age*, 664.

16. For an example, see the analytic philosophy of "eliminative materialism" as espoused by Churchland, *Computational Brain*.

done."[17] Incessant deadlines, productivity demands, quarterly reports, outcome assessments, and accelerating technological change (with built-in planned obsolescence), drive us ever onwards, until our time runs out. Our leisure, increasingly melded into our work time, counts on a cascade of trends launched by charismatic influencers or by algorithms that feed the mediascape consumption of entertainment, sports, and memes.

Life, so construed, becomes intolerably empty for some. For just as there are people who do not fit in to cultures dominated by religion, misfits spin off from contemporary secular cultures too. They may submit to the rule of clock time, work as required, and participate in the prevailing enchantments, yet they cannot shake the sense that something that should be paramount to life has gone missing. Nothing in the news or in the cultural scheme of things fully explains this malaise. Those who feel it can't block the sense that somewhere there must be a fullness that transcends what people normally talk about and ordinarily care about. Stated another way, they have an intuition that "there are more things in heaven and earth than are dreamt of on Wall Street or in Silicon Valley."[18]

One all-around misfit—in this case, an outsider to both religious and secular orders—is the Danish writer Soren Kierkegaard (1813–55). He is one of the first thinkers in the Western world to fully grasp the consequences of the loss of depth and of existential urgency in the modern world. At odds with both the half-baked Christendom of his day and the flattening of time to progressive *chronos*, he spent a good deal of his short life trying to uncover our awareness of, and our relation to, eternity. In an early work, *Fear and Trembling* (1843), Kierkegaard's pseudonym, Johannes de silentio, asks: "If there were no eternal consciousness in a man, if at the bottom of everything there were only a wild ferment . . . if an unfathomable, insatiable emptiness lay hid beneath everything, what would life be but despair?"[19] According to Kierkegaard, we

17. Taylor, *Secular Age*, 59.
18. McCarraher, *Enchantments of Mammon*, 18.
19. Kierkegaard, *Fear and Trembling*, 14.

Chapter Four: When the Light Gets In

become "tranquilized by the trivial."[20] In many ways we are actually in a condition of despair, whether we happen to know it or not.

Before turning further to Kierkegaard, it is worth noting that with both Nietzsche and Kierkegaard, we are looking at lives that were anything but normal. Though they are studied extensively today, there was a strangeness in their works that placed them outside the dominant views of their day. The life stories of both are marked by extremity, which leads many commentators to explain their ideas solely in terms of the devastating events that shook them. Granted, the early, horrific death of Nietzsche's father, Nietzsche's own debilitating medical condition, and his eventual fall into hereditary madness cannot be neatly separated from his writings. In the case of Kierkegaard, the oppressiveness of his father (who was burdened by the memory of cursing God as a boy), the death of multiple siblings, and his physical oddities—his curved spine made him an object of mockery in Copenhagen—factor into his life story and his *oeuvre*. Yet in trying to understand Nietzsche and Kierkegaard, it is easy to get distracted by their controversial biographies and miss their call to focus on what is means to be alive. With these thinkers, we do well to bear in mind Northrop Frye's observation that "it is not only, perhaps not even primarily, the balanced and judicious people that we turn to for insight." Adding Nietzsche and Kierkegaard to a list with Baudelaire, Rimbaud, Hölderlin, and Dostoevsky, Frye notes that "they were people whose lives got smashed up in various ways, but rescued fragments from the smash of an intensity that the steady-state people seldom get to hear about."[21] One such "fragment" in Nietzsche's work is the concept of "the transvaluation of values," his great insight that ossified moral laws kill our creative instincts and

---

20. Quoted in Becker, *Denial of Death*, 80.

21. Frye, *Collected Works*, 4:39–40. To my mind, William James makes the same point when he writes, "There is no doubt that healthy mindedness is inadequate as a philosophical doctrine, because the evil facts which it positively refuses to account for are a genuine portion of reality; and they may after all be the very best key to life's significance, and possibly the only openers of our eyes to the deepest levels of truth." See *Varieties of Religious Experience*, Lectures VI and VII, "The Sick Soul" (117).

desires. A related idea, conveyed in aphorisms, is that a hidden impulse to domination underlies the vaunted power of Western reason, an impulse, Nietzsche predicted, would lead to coming world conflicts marked by the "monstrous logic of terror."[22] In the case of Kierkegaard, assorted remarks of his various pseudonyms gather into a breakthrough understanding of the subjective dimension of knowledge. Kierkegaard's concepts funded the twentieth-century philosophies of phenomenology and existentialism, while preceding their formulations by a century.

Kierkegaard's clash with the steady-state citizens of Denmark has both secular and religious aspects. While he is best known for his religious critique of established Christianity in nineteenth-century Denmark, this critique stems from observations that are sociological in part. Above all, he recognized the power of social conformity. Pressure to conform generates mass society, the phenomenon Kierkegaard called "the crowd." "The crowd is untruth"[23] is one of his better-known exhortations. (If Kierkegaard were to become a commodity of sorts, this is the slogan that a niche marketing strategy would put on the t-shirt.) His point is that we are born into standardized expectations and absorbed by cultural customs, those dominant ways of doing things that go without saying. Prevailing habits of mind lead people to adopt ready-made identities and to subscribe to the dominant interpretation of what life is all about.

Kierkegaard's insights into social conditioning go beyond his own time and place. Today, if you read a classic study of American life in the 1950s—for example, David Riseman's *The Lonely Crowd* or C. Wright Mills's *White Collar*—it's hard not to think of Kierkegaard's prescient grasp of the nature of modern conformity. And while Kierkegaard did not develop a full-blown theory of conformism, he might well have agreed with René Girard's

---

22. Michael Allen Gillespie discusses this prescient aspect of Nietzsche's thought in *Nietzsche's Final Teaching*, 22 and 192. Nietzsche calls for the "revaluation of all values" in the conclusion to *The Antichrist* (1895).

23. Kierkegaard, *Point of View for My Work as an Author*, introduction and 112.

Chapter Four: When the Light Gets In

late twentieth-century idea of *mimesis*. On this view, people are inclined to do what everybody else is doing because, beyond basic needs, our desires and emotions are learned from others in and through lifelong imitation. The problem, Kierkegaard realized, is that when everyone is copying everyone else and everything is already understood by others, there's no impetus to ask unsettling questions.

Kierkegaard's insights into human culture and behavior focus on the public and on the media. In "The Present Age," he critiques the idea of the general public, whose lauded general opinion he considers to be a "monstrous abstraction." Distinguishing the *public*, as a conglomerate of undifferentiated persons, from genuine *community*, he attacks the public's capacity for "leveling."[24] By "levelling" Kierkegaard does not mean the diminishment of class hierarchy. Some commentators assume as much given Kierkegaard's conservative political temperament. Rather, by "leveling" he means the reduction of all information to one-dimensionality, the equation of the most trivial things with matters of existential consequence.

Kierkegaard's attack on the notion of the public zeroes in on *anonymity*. He thinks the desire to be anonymous arises largely from emerging media, namely, the burgeoning newspapers of his day. As with digital social media today, he could see that the popular press was undercutting the human capacity for face-to-face communicative encounters. And he knew the difference firsthand. While caricatures of Kierkegaard sometimes depict him as a sequestered figure trembling with anxiety in a lonely room, actually his daily routine involved long walks through the streets of Copenhagen when he would strike up conversations as he went. This routine ended, however, when he became the object of mockery in the tabloid newspaper, *The Corsair*. While Kierkegaard provoked this attack in part, becoming a public laughingstock led him to see how people treat others differently when they are acting and reacting anonymously. In short, a person's viewpoint degenerates when it is

---

24. Kierkegaard discusses the bloodless abstraction of the public and "leveling" in "The Present Age," an essay in Kierkegaard, *Two Ages*, 87.

immersed in the impersonal expression of mass media. Corrosion of the capacity for self-reflection sets in. Kierkegaard states the gist of the matter in his *Journal*: "no one wants to be *I* but pulls in his antennae and becomes third person, 'the public, they.'"[25]

SELF AND ETERNITY

For Kierkegaard, shrinking from the "I" leads to the loss of human selfhood. And with selfhood effaced, the capacity for personal transformation falls away. On the everyday social surface, this loss might not even be noticed. But from Kierkegaard's theological perspective, it means something ultimately important has died.[26] When personal agency becomes submerged in the conformity of the crowd, a person's inward possibility for eternal happiness goes too. Why this is so Kierkegaard is at pains to convey. In the multifaceted body of works composed over his enigmatic life, his purpose is, no less, to disclose the possibility of the individual's opening to the experience of sacred joy.

Kierkegaard's view of the nature of the human self focuses on existential factors, our mortality above all. In philosophical argot, his view of human selfhood foregrounds the ontological reality of existence as prior to epistemological queries. Unlike Descartes, who first fashioned a rational method to show that the self can have certain knowledge, or the British empiricists (Locke and Hume), for whom sense-experience provided a basis for what we know, or Kant, who thought reality fits our minds, Kierkegaard stresses the uncertainty of human knowing. His starting point is more in tune with Hegel, for whom the *relational* structure of human selfhood is axiomatic. That is, the essential feature of human consciousness— what makes us different from other animals—is *self-consciousness*. Moreover, we become aware of ourselves as self-conscious beings

---

25. Kierkegaard, *Journals and Papers*, entry no. 2075.
26. As Kierkegaard puts it into *Sickness Unto Death*, "In the world, the greatest danger, that of losing one's self, can occur so quietly that it is as if it were nothing at all. No other loss can take place so quietly; every other loss— an arm, a leg, five rixdollrs, a spouse, etc.—is noticed, however" (43).

Chapter Four: When the Light Gets In

in relation to other self-conscious beings. The dialectic at the core of this process—perceiving another and in being perceived—engenders our communicability and gives rise to our capacity for self-reflection as creatures of both body and spirit.

Kierkegaard splits from Hegel as he develops his distinctive view of the human self. He shows how deepening self-reflection can lead us beyond petty thoughts and pointless projects. As we grow in our capacity for freedom, we can cast off the false self. We awaken to see ourselves as individuals rather than the social roles we play.[27] Instead of adopting a fixed identity, authentic self-appropriation fosters increasing awareness of life's possibilities. Yet here, in the midst of this interior growth, a problem arises, and its consequences for human selfhood are immense. For the very freedom that nurtures awareness of possibility can also give rise to profound dread. In other words, "dizzying" insecurity comes bundled with our freedom of choice. A crisis of meaning follows. In his *Journal*, Kierkegaard likens the experience to finding oneself swimming over "70,000 fathoms of water." In *The Concept of Anxiety*, the roots and contours of this experience are laid bare. One of Kierkegaard's commentators, Michael Watts, depicts the experience this way:

> [Anxiety] can arise anytime, anywhere, without warning. For instance, I may be taking a quiet walk in the countryside when out of the blue, as if from nowhere, the suffocating feeling of the pointlessness of everything overwhelms me. Life suddenly appears utterly senseless—all ambition seems futile and achievements shrink into insignificance as I am confronted with the unlimited possibilities facing me, including my own demise. I find myself staring directly into the void of nothingness—the inevitability of my death.... This strange feeling of dread,

---

27. See Aroosi, *Dialectical Self*. Aroosi provides an extended examination of the complexities in Kierkegaard's view of the self, while also showing how Kierkegaard both draws upon and attacks Hegel's formulations. Entire books have been written on Kierkegaard's relation to Hegel, and many studies of Kierkegaard center around his use of pseudonyms and his method of "indirect communication." For the purposes of my limited discussion here, I am summarizing key points.

that one's consciousness will one day be completely and permanently terminated . . . cannot be compared to any other form of human experience.[28]

We rely on psychological repression to keep the terror of this experience at bay. We may avoid many uncomfortable thoughts in our daily lives, but none runs so deep. In a meditative piece entitled "At a Graveside," Kierkegaard reflects on the "innumerable evasions" that we use to flee awareness of death—not death in general, but our own.[29] He finds that most people will stay busy enough to avoid thinking about death at all. Or they will find some way to dismiss it, like the Stoic philosopher Epicurus, who famously claimed that death is inconsequential since at the time of death we won't actually experience our own non-being.[30] It's not a big deal, as my student would say. Kierkegaard's position, by contrast, has more in common with the poet Philip Larkin, who in his poem, "Aubade," calls death awareness "a special way of being afraid / No trick dispels."[31]

But Kierkegaard's likeness to Larkin goes no farther than spotting the "tricks" and "evasions" of death denial. The "special way of being afraid" becomes, for Kierkegaard, the threshold to religious awakening. Death must be confronted, but when seriously faced, and when the overall significance of our life comes into irrevocable view, a path to meaning arrives. In Kierkegaard's paradoxical formulation, "To know oneself in one's nothingness is the condition for knowing God"[32]—where, full stop, it is vital to note that Kierkegaard means God as the ground and abyss of being, and not as *a* supreme being. In terms of selfhood, to discover one's death as a subjective truth, and not as something in general, is to create the self that had been invisible before. It is to rediscover ourselves in relation to the eternal—"the eternal, from which we

28. Watts, *Kierkegaard*, 161.

29. The 1845 discourse "At a Graveside" appears as the third of *Three Discourses on Imagined Occasions*, 69–102.

30. Epicurus, "Letter to Menoeceus" 156–57.

31. Larkin, *Collected Poems*, 190.

32. Kierkegaard, *Eighteen Upbuilding Discourses*, 321.

CHAPTER FOUR: WHEN THE LIGHT GETS IN

come and to which we go, and which gives us *to* ourselves and liberates us *from* ourselves."[33] This is not eternity in the sense of an afterlife, but rather as the gift of being, now in this life, in the preciousness of each present moment.

ETERNITY AND LOVE

Kierkegaard's view that our true self is born through an encounter with nothingness points up the apophatic strain in his theology. In terms I have been using in this study, it's the side of his thought that gives the negative—"the nothing that interlaces existence," as he calls it—its unrelenting due. As Peter Kline states in *Passion for Nothing: Kierkegaard's Apophatic Theology*, Kierkegaard understands faith as an "existential exigency,"[34] an ongoing openness of the self to the paradox of the eternal in time. Faith is not unquestioning adherence to a confessional identity propped up by religious behavior. Kierkegaard's approach aims at *relationality* above all, a transformation that occurs not by assuming a religious identity but by undertaking a living response to a call—a call that only comes in fully facing that we will die.[35] Only in grasping that we will lose our lives can we glimpse the ultimate significance of our lives. Faith then becomes a movement forward into the unknown. What's vital in this movement is what Kierkegaard calls "the passion of the infinite" in the unending task of becoming spirit.

Kierkegaard's account of our relationship to eternity focuses on the individual. This focus finds clear expression in *Fear and Trembling* where Kierkegaard's pseudonym, Johannes de silentio, maintains that "the individual is higher than the universal."[36]

33. Tillich, *Eternal Now*, 46.

34. Kline, *Passion for Nothing*, 2. The phrase "the nothing that interlaces existence" is from *Either / Or*, 1:291.

35. As Kierkegaard states in *For Self-Examination and Judge for Yourself*, "Christianity teaches that you must die. Your power must be dismantled. And the life-giving spirit is the one who slays you" (76).

36. Kierkegaard's pseudonym Johannes de silentio claims that "the individual is higher than the universal" in *Fear and Trembling / Repetition*, 55.

Given this singular focus, Kierkegaard's claim to be indifferent to politics is unsurprising. And yet, his focus on the private self is not impermeable. For one thing, Kierkegaard's attacks on ecclesiastical authority and "Christendom" are hardly signs of someone with no irons in the sociopolitical fires of his day. Further, the purely personal mold is broken in one key book: *Works of Love*. In this book, Kierkegaard develops a treatise on love, a theological argument that fleshes out of the social dimension of selfhood. Yet it's not social theory that prompts this theologian to write *Works of Love*. For Kierkegaard, it is the double love commandment of Jesus: "You shall love the Lord God," and further, "You shall love your neighbor as yourself" (Matt 22:37–39).

Finding one's true subjectivity in relation to the eternal does not occur in a silo. *Works of Love* makes the case that such spiritual development entails relating to our fellow humans beyond their social roles. This requires love, but not the kind that, underneath it all, is really empathy, or only the seeming-sort of love based on self-interest, or on taste, or on favoritism towards those with whom we prefer to associate. For one with ears to hear, the biblical directive is to love the neighbor *simply because he or she is the neighbor*. As Jennifer Veninga puts it, "Kierkegaard's neighbor-love stresses recognizing the universal worth and dignity of all people."[37] Since faith means accepting a love that unconditionally loves us, we are summoned to recognize, uphold, and value human differences and the irreducible singularity of every person. As Kierkegaard states, "In being king, beggar, rich man, poor man, male, female, etc., we are not like each other—therein we are indeed different. But in being neighbor we are all unconditionally like each other."[38]

Kierkegaard declares "No, politics is not for me" in *Letters and Documents*. Quoted by Marino in his Forward to *Kierkegaard and Political Theology*, xiii.

37. Veninga, "Loving the Ones We See," 119.
38. Kierkegaard, *Works of Love*, 89.

Chapter Four: When the Light Gets In

ETERNITY AND JUSTICE

From his principle that "the neighbor is eternity's mark on every human being," Kierkegaard could conjure a vision of genuine community. But while such a vision provided a corrective to the "crowd" he so disdained, it does not speak sufficiently to our situation today. The social world of early nineteenth-century Denmark offers no model for understanding the systematized poverty and exploitation that millions on our planet face now. As Gordon Marino points out, while Kierkegaard may offer loving counsel to the dispossessed and the downtrodden in *Works of Love*, he "did not experience any urgency about the necessity of implementing a more equal distribution of wealth, rights, and opportunities."[39] In our own time, when the economic interests of a small and privileged group of humans rule whole populations on our desacralized earth, we need a pertinent formulation of the principle of love. We need the insight and promise articulated by Cornel West: "justice is what love looks like in public."[40]

With these words, West proclaims another biblical principle, namely, the prophetic. As discussed in chapter 1, this is the standpoint of the Hebrew prophets who witnessed to the suffering of their people and called for righteousness on their behalf. Prophetic critique is a cry against the injustices of the ruling elites, economic, political, and religious. In our own day, it strives to be heard across multiple cultures. It has risen in the wake of centuries of colonialism tied to the empire building of the Western powers. Prophetic critique today is further complicated by the global factor of man-made climate change and the exploitation of resources on a planetary scale. In the wake of neoliberalism as the continuation of imperialist hegemony through predatory capitalism, the demand for reimagined social justice must look beyond the good intentions of pious souls.

---

39. Marino, "Foreword," xiv.

40. West, "Justice Is What Love Looks Like in Public," Sermon at Howard University.

Next to Nothing

A host of theologians have responded to this demand and they have heard the call for prophetic critique befitting our era. One example is the British theologian, Herbert McCabe (1926–2001), who, in 1980, disturbed the relatively calm waters of conservative Christianity in the United Kingdom with the publication of a seminal essay, "The Class Struggle and Christian Love." This essay lays bare the destructive antagonism inherent in rampant consumerist economies. Rejecting the ideology of greed—the idol of the Capitalocene—McCabe argues for the meaning and necessity of class struggle in light of the Christian imperative of universal love. He points out that "Christianity is deeply subversive of capitalism precisely because it announces the improbable possibility that men might live together without war, neither by domination nor by antagonism but by unity in love."[41]

Another prophetic figure is Oscar Romero (1917–80), the former archbishop of San Salvador. He was a conservative theologian who, for many years, stayed in step with the traditional priorities of the Roman Catholic magisterium. Initially, his ministry did not place him at odds with the hierarchy of the Salvadorian military government. But after witnessing the discrimination and violence systematically unleashed upon the poorest classes of his nation—as well as the murder of a friend who was helping the marginalized—Romero's theological outlook radically changed. He decided to live in solidarity with the oppressed. With this change, he did not lose his belief in the personally transforming nature of love. Rather, he came to view love in a wider social context. And, as is often the case when such persons speak out, he was killed outright for taking a prophetic stand. In the sermon preached just minutes before his assassination by a right-wing death squad, he said, "One must not love oneself so much as to avoid getting involved in the risks of life that history demands of us. . . ."[42]

Prophetic men and women have come to light in world faiths and in indigenous religions. In the Christian faith, the pioneering

---

41. McCabe, "Class Struggle," 182–98. For the term "Capitalocene" I am indebted to Rieger, *Theology in the Capitalocene*, 2–3.

42. Quoted in Wirzba, *Way of Love*, 6.

CHAPTER FOUR: WHEN THE LIGHT GETS IN

model of prophetic ministry is the life of Jesus of Nazareth. He lived in the first century of the Common Era in the eastern part of the Roman Empire then known as Palestine. As modern scholarship has made clear, Jesus did not view himself as the divine founder of a new religion called "Christianity."[43] Jesus worshiped in local synagogues, but also at the large temple complex in Jerusalem. Within the varied streams of the Jewish tradition, he lived out the consequences of the prophetic principle that God acts in history, and first and foremost, that God had changed the course of history by standing in solidarity with exploited slaves in Egypt. Jesus's ministry was based on free healing and communal meals. He lived in proximity with the large underclass of peasants and in solidarity with those excluded by the powerful. He was, in effect, a nonviolent resistance leader who clashed with dominant hierarchies on two fronts, as recounted in the New Testament (and other) Gospels. On the one hand, Jesus confronted and criticized the wealthy Jewish authorities who ran the temple. To protest the fiscal and sacrificial practices of the Holy City's high priests, he occupied the temple, as depicted in Mark 11:11–17. But through this symbolic act of incursion, he was also indicting their comfortable collaboration with Roman imperial authorities. Jesus's own confrontation with Roman authorities was more perilous, given the police state's prompt and extensive use of crucifixion; this method of torture and execution was the Romans' chief means for controlling the populace through public displays of genocidal terror. Yet, when his enemies laid a political trap for him on the question of paying taxes to the Empire, his well-known rejoinder—"Render to Caesar the things that are Caesar's and to God the things that are God's" (Mark 12:15–17)—served to challenge both the slave-based economy and the divine sanction of Roman rule. In this act, as Bruce Chilton puts it, Jesus "contrasted Roman coins and the

---

43. For a fuller discussion of Jesus's prophetic life in its socio-historical setting, see Borg, *Meeting Jesus Again for the First Time*; Crossan, *Jesus*; Rohr, *Universal Christ*. I am also indebted to *The Norton Anthology of World Religions: Christianity*, and to McFague, *Speaking in Parables*.

artificial image of Caesar on them . . . with what was owed to God as the source of humanity itself."[44]

As Jesus taught in a defeated backwater of the Roman Empire, he addressed people in part through parables. In place of harangues, he told imaginative stories. That he delivered teachings in parables is striking, but perhaps not surprising when we consider the unique features of this literary form. Recognizing that *modern* authors also write parables, the biblical scholar, C. H. Dodd, in 1935, arrived at a definition of the parable form that remains salient to this day. A parable, according to Dodd, is "a metaphor or simile drawn from nature or common life, arresting the hearer by its vividness or strangeness, and leaving the mind in sufficient doubt about its precise application to tease it into active thought."[45] Defined as such, a parable is distinguishable from an allegory. An allegory is a literary device intended to be grasped as a single idea or applied as a moral dictum. By contrast, as the narrative images of a parable unfold, double meanings are evoked and participatory interpretation ensues. Parables have mundane elements in being drawn from "common life," as Dodd says, yet they can also carry an extravagant message. With their capacity for double meanings and openness to interpretation, parables can be both subversive and revelatory. In short, the parable was well suited to the double-edged disclosures of the kind Jesus was making. His stories reflect a subversive stance towards dominant powers, but they also offer an alternative world to the world molded and policed by Empire.

Jesus's stories use familiar details about ordinary people engaged in seemingly secular decisions, but through that mundanity a surprising reversal of expectations occurs that opens up a new way of discerning our relationship to God. The parable of the Good Samaritan (Luke 10:30–35) is a case in point. Jesus's story

44. Chilton, *Herods*, 243.

45. Dodd, *Parables of the Kingdom*, 5. For my own study of the confluence between ancient and modern parables, see Champion, "Parable as an Ancient and Modern Form," 16–39. My thesis: "Awareness of this genre's elasticity has coincided with the discovery that the metaphorical, paradoxical, and confrontative qualities of New Testament parables are also to be found within the vast range of contemporary literature" (22).

Chapter Four: When the Light Gets In

recounts how a man going down the road fell among robbers who strip him and beat him and depart. Having seen the half-dead victim by the side of the road, first one man—a priest—and then another—a Levite—pass by on the other side. But then a third man does stop to help the wounded traveler. This third man—a Samaritan—goes to the traumatized victim. He "bandaged his wounds, having poured oil and wine on them. Then he put him on his own animal, brought him to an inn and took care of him. The next day he took out two denarii, gave them to the innkeeper, and said, 'Take care of him; and when I come back, I will repay you whatever more you spend.'"[46]

At one level, this is an *example* story. It provides an illustration of the compassion religious people should exercise. The third man's actions show how you ought to love your neighbor. Go and do likewise. But there's more. At another level, this story is a critique of the purity system dominating society in early first-century Israel, the exclusionary laws established in the wake of the long history of animosity between Jews and disdained outsiders like Samaritans. In other words, by depicting a sullied Samaritan as having mercy, and not the more respected figures of a priest and Levite, the story in effect deconstructs a way of life ordered around ethnic prejudices and hierarchal gradations of purity.

At a deeper level still, the Good Samaritan is a parable for anyone with ears to interpret. If the telling has provoked "active thought," as Dodd puts it, then we have been challenged to think in a new way. From this angle, the third man's actions point to the nature of God as radically imminent, as present in the concrete lives of persons acting in the material world.

In the Synoptic Gospels and in Paul's theology, a primary metaphor for divine presence is the "kingdom of God." In Mark's Gospel, for example, Jesus says the kingdom of God "is like a mustard seed, which, when sown upon the ground, is the smallest of all the seeds on earth; yet when it is sown it grows up and becomes the greatest of all shrubs, and puts forth large branches, so that the birds of the air can make nests in its shade" (Mark 4:30–32).

---

46. This is Crossan's translation in *Power of Parable*, 48.

But why would Jesus use the phrase "kingdom of God" when the word "kingdom" evokes the epitome of hierarchical rule, the antithesis of his egalitarian teachings? As New Testament scholar John Dominic Crossan notes, just as the surprising conjunction of mustard seed and kingdom makes more sense when the context of Mediterranean mustard plant is brought into consideration,[47] the term "kingdom of God" is best understood to as a performative metaphor, as a counterpoint to and confrontation with the kingdom of Julius Caesar. It lays bare the contrast between the presence of God and the reign of Rome. In short, some words and images that appear in the stories of Jesus and stories about Jesus were chosen for their direct opposition to Roman rule. The imperial machinations of Rome were fueled by incessant propaganda, including proclamations that Caesar Augustus was God incarnate, the Savior of the world, and, strikingly, the Son of God.[48] By contrast, the kingdom of God, open to the disenfranchised of the earth, exposes the narcissistic delusions of tyrants and turns upside down the values of conquest, patriarchy, and slavery. The kingdom of God is the promise of distributive justice and hope for "the least of these" (Matt 25:45).

47. Crossan provides context for understanding the mustard seed metaphor. In *Jesus*, Crossan writes, "a word about Mediterranean mustard plants and nesting birds helps us to understand the startling nature of that conjunction. . . . There is . . . a distinction between the wild mustard and its domesticated counterpart, but even when one deliberately cultivates the latter for its medicinal or culinary properties, there is an ever-present danger that it will destroy the garden. The mustard plant is dangerous even when domesticated in the garden, and is deadly when growing wild in the grain fields. . . . The point . . . is not just that the mustard plant starts as a proverbially small seed and grows to a shrub of three, four, or even more feet in height. It's that it tends to take over where it is not wanted, and it tends to get out of control, and it tends to attract birds within cultivated areas where they are not particularly desired. And that, said Jesus, was what the Kingdom was like" (64–65).

48. Crossan makes this point in *Power of the Parable*, 158. Crossan's many insights stem from his rich understanding of Jesus within the matrix of the Roman Empire. It is the essential background to understanding Jesus in the same way, as he notes, "the matrix for Gandhi is British imperialism, and that for Martin Luther King Jr. is American racism." See *How to Read the Bible and Still Be a Christian*, 236.

Chapter Four: When the Light Gets In

The kingdom metaphor has suffused prophetic visions throughout history. The realization that the kingdom of God "is already here," as Jesus states in Mark 1:1–15, has inspired men and women to challenge corrupt colonial systems that maintain retributive justice through violence and the apparatuses of punishment and death. To take this stance is very often to risk "disappearance." But it is also to participate in the power of justice breaking down barriers—the barriers, for example, of class, race, gender, and tribe as announced in Gal 3:28: "There is no longer Jew or Greek, there is no longer slave or free, there is no longer male and female, for all of you are one in Christ Jesus."

The prophetic stance arises from the capacity to imagine alternative ways of being in the world based on justice and love of neighbor. As Walter Brueggemann has noted in his classic book, *The Prophetic Imagination*, when it comes to struggling for justice, "the imagination must come before the implementation."[49] Imaginative metaphors are, hence, enormously consequential in the multiple ways they shape world views. For example, turning from the ancient world to the modern world, consider how two ascendent metaphors shaped hearts and minds amid the world-wide financial crisis leading up to World War II. As astute historians have pointed out, the struggle between fascism and democratic socialism in the 1930s was, at one level, a clash between the metaphors of Reich and New Deal. The Reich metaphor envisioned an authoritarian national state directed by a Fuhrer, where the New Deal envisioned a democracy rooted in the essential equality of persons.

In expectation of what human life could be, prophetic visions in both religious and secularized formats invoke metaphors, symbols, and images that point to a possible "commonwealth" of peace and justice. At the same time, they warn of the lure of ideologies that offer a false sense of security in the face of current existential crises. This combination of hope and critique is conditioned by the realities of a particular historical moment. The parables of Jesus, for example, reflect his place and time and a society split between

---

49. Brueggemann, *Prophetic Imagination*, 40.

very rich and very poor. To jump again from the ancient to the modern world, prophetic movements today have come into focus around an all-pervasive issue: impending climate disaster. For decades, persons intimately attuned to the land and persons who could read the scientific writing on the wall have been trying to alert the human race to the ecological calamity that threatens the entire planet. For example, in 1962, Rachel Carson's *Silent Spring* warned that synthetic pesticides were causing environmental havoc—a warning, by the way, that prompted chemical companies initially to attack her work as foolish. A more recent example is Greta Thunberg's speech in 2019 before the UN Climate Action Summit in which she pointed out that "entire eco-systems are collapsing" under the dominant delusion of "eternal economic growth."[50] Thunberg's fiery words drew significant media attention. She even appeared on the cover of *Time* magazine. But as often as not the attention shifted to her young age or her "heroic" struggle with Aspergers, while failing to heed the scientific evidence she had presented. Such deflections of the urgency of prophetic warnings are not new. However, the scope of the call by Thunberg and others for environmental justice is unprecedented. It is now abundantly clear that any attempts to envision a viable future must begin with awareness that social and environmental justice are inextricably entwined.

---

50. Quoted in Beal, *When Time Is Short*, 126. Beal's view of the reaction to Thunberg's speech matches my own. Beal writes, "What I mostly see is how quickly we shift the focus away from [Thunberg's] hard words and onto her remarkable courage and exceptional talents as an individual." As willful blindness goes, a related point is that the refusal to face human-caused climate change is long-running, as documented in Shannon Hall's article in *Scientific American*, "Exxon Knew About Climate Change Almost 40 Years Ago." Hall writes, "Exxon was aware of climate change, as early as 1977, 11 years before it became a public issue. . . . This knowledge did not prevent the company (now ExxonMobil and the world's largest oil and gas company) from spending decades refusing to acknowledge climate change and even promoting climate misinformation."

Chapter Four: When the Light Gets In

٭

To recall the title of this chapter, prophetic expectations and the struggles for justice can be viewed as instances when "the light" gets in. But to perceive the cracks that allow in the light entails facing the immensity of the darkness that surrounds them. For those called to prophetic utterance, it means giving voice as well to the condition of loss. It means grieving what is irretrievably gone. And it means knowing that when the kingdom of God breaks through in history, hope remains brittle. The restoration of distributive justice is temporary. Tyranny, rampant greed, authoritarian lies, and willful ignorance return—often making use of and distorting the very tools that were used to overcome them. For example, at this writing, white supremacists in America, intent on spreading hatred, deploy the right to "free speech," which, in the past, has served as a catalyst of anti-fascist democracy. Evil rebounds, in other words, as if on cue. Then large questions loom, as they always have. If the kingdom of God is not a final, supernaturally staged event, but rather, a reality here now as we work for it in divine-human collaboration, are the breakthroughs of the kingdom in time more than fleeting? How can we both acknowledge the tragic limits of humanity while also embracing mutuality and the call for social justice? The following chapter looks to further symbols of the manifestations of the eternal in time.

Chapter Five: Kairos Calling

> ... how strange it is to be anything at all. —Neutral Milk Hotel, "In the Aeroplane Over the Sea"[1]

> God is the name for the rift which involves the human being in a choice concerning the meaning of its being. —David J. Kangas[2]

> I had never known, never even imagined for a heartbeat, that there might be a place for people like us. —Denis Johnson[3]

LITERATURE PROVIDES A PORTAL to the depth dimension of our lives. For example, Hamlet's "to be or not to be" speech can still speak to our need for a reason to live, though the play was composed over four centuries ago. Contemporary readers who stay with Melville's demanding *Moby Dick* can find their imaginative horizons expanding when "the great flood-gates of the wonder world" begin to open for Ishmael. And if literary works can question life and evoke wonder, they also have the capacity to explore human limits. The ancient epic of *Gilgamesh* and Tolstoy's short story about Ivan Ilyich are at hand to lay bare the intricacies of the human drive to deny death. In a more positive vein, Toni Morrison leads readers into an astonishing moment of radical grace in the

---

1. Neutral Milk Hotel, "In the Aeroplane Over the Sea," lyrics by Jeff Mangum from the album *In the Aeroplane Over the Sea*, Merge Records, 1998.
2. Kangas, *Errant Affirmations*, 130.
3. Johnson, *Jesus' Son*, 133.

Chapter Five: Kairos Calling

Clearing scene of *Beloved*, though the breakthrough comes in the midst of a harrowing tale.[4]

There are many facets to the depth dimension that great literature reveals, for literary works can be political, emotional, social, educational, aesthetic, spiritual—and ontological too. If our lives are never not a mixture of being and non-being, literary works stand out in their capacity to depict our lives and our milieus as entanglements of creative and destructive powers. On occasion, this entanglement may be disclosed in abstract terms, as in Wallace Stevens's poem, "The Snow Man," where the wintery mind of a "listener" in the snow "beholds / Nothing that is not there and the nothing that is." Or the ontological factors that underscore human life may be noted in a humorous aside, as when the narrator of Flannery O'Connor's story, "Parker's Back," tells readers that "Parker had never before felt the least motion of wonder in himself. . . . It did not enter his head that there was anything out of the ordinary about the fact that he existed." The truth of what we are can be hidden, and it can also cut into our lives in moments of epiphany, as deep-running meaning appears and goes. For example, when Virginia Woolf's character, Mrs. Dalloway, learns at her party about the suicide of World War I veteran, Septimus Smith, something ultimate startles her, if only for an instant. In the midst of her stream of consciousness, and surrounded as it is by "corruption, lies, chatter," for a moment she knows: "a thing there was that mattered."[5]

The ontological insights in imaginative literature and in a wide range of cultural creations should inform theology. As theologian David Tracy has said, theology is too important to be left to theologians.[6] For if it is to be more than the preservation of doctrine, and if it is to escape authoritarian drift, it must begin with the human condition. This means, on the one hand, that theology

---

4. Shakespeare, *Hamlet*, Act 3, Scene 1; Melville, *Moby-Dick*, chapter 1: "Loomings"; Morrison, *Beloved*, chapter 9.

5. Stevens, *Collected Poems*, 10; O'Connor, "Parker's Back," 513; Woolf, *Mrs. Dalloway*, 184.

6. Tracy, *Filaments*, 215.

can turn to the human imagination with its capacity to create and to receive symbols that give rise to meaning. On the other hand, theology must dive beneath the troubled surface of our reality with its pervasive loss and despair, for only the honest portrayal of our situation occasions the possibility of moving beyond it.

Throughout this study I have used the term "apophatic" in a broadened sense. Like the word "existential," which once meant something technical in philosophy but is now used in other arenas like political science—it can even be heard on the evening news—the term *apophatic* now references more than an arcane strain of mystical thought. While not an everyday word, its usage is growing. For example, a recent article in the *Journal of the American Academy of Religion* employs the term "apophatic" in formulating an innovative method of interpretation.[7] A further example is the practice of centering prayer, which has grown in mainline churches in recent years. The emphasis on silence and on awareness of absence in this practice has led to new understanding of the apophatic tradition in the West, as well as its affinities with Eastern meditative forms. In short, the term "apophatic" has gained cogency as a heuristic lens, as an orientation that honors absence and doubt and unknowing as part and parcel with profound faith.

To reiterate, I have been motivated in this study to give non-being its due by recognizing the unrelenting loss that striates our lifeworld. At the same time, non-being can be seen as the catalyst for the power of being that heals and transforms us. Chapter 1 outlines the contours of an apophatic theology. Chapter 2 defines the kind of knowledge intrinsic to it. Chapter 3 focuses on the power of non-being as it is addressed by religion, but also as it suffuses and distorts religion itself. Chapter 4 seeks openings to moments when we encounter the eternal as individuals and, no less, in the struggle for social justice. The present chapter spotlights Christian symbols, including creation and cross, but also, and what is more important than any symbol or doctrine, the meaning-bearing power of love.

---

7. Tolstaya and Bestebreurtje, "Furthering the Dialogue," 469–505.

Chapter Five: Kairos Calling

While I am aware that many thoughtful people today would prefer to wash their hands of religion altogether, with Christianity often placed first in line for expungement, other options are beckoning. Understanding the life we have been given in relation to the sacred is one goal we can envision. Despite the juggernaut of fundamentalism, we may be living in a liminal time when that goal is available, a time when old dispensations of religion—the kind that excluded the secular—are falling away. Stated another way, we may be reaching an historical juncture when secular modes of thought are awakening to the need for . . . what to name it? Call it "spirituality," perhaps, or call it by any name that designates an opening to the hidden side of our lives, an opening that finds expression and form when we encounter an uncanny "place," the unfathomable nothing from which we have come, the *prius* of our natality, and the no-thing-ness to which our mortality is taking us. As we speak, so the saying goes.

CREATION

Being as such is good. Cataphatic theology tells us so. God's power of being is creative. It is the divine eros or love at work in the world. At the same time, it is the power of diversity and relationship, and it entails the meaningful self-affirmation of every being. "Spirit is the wind from God that is sweeping across the cosmos, creating and calling."[8]

The first creation story in the Bible inaugurates these points. God creates an orderly world of heaven and earth. In the second verse of the opening chapter of Genesis, the creation takes place as "the wind from God swept over the face of the waters" (Gen 1:2). However, one might ask, how did the waters get there? Like other ancient peoples, the Hebrews believed the world was founded on pre-existent, formless matter. As in several creation myths, this preexistent, chaotic matter is water. For example, in the Sumerian myth, the still and primordial ocean of chaos is personified as the

---

8. Hodgson, *Winds of the Spirit*, 175.

goddess Nammu, who gives "birth to heaven and earth." In the Babylonian creation epic, *Enuma Elish*, the chaos is made up of both fresh and salt water, and Marduk creates heaven and earth from the salt water.

In the third century CE, Christian theologians sought to address the problem of Genesis' preexistent water. For the Christian belief that God caused everything clearly clashed with the biblical story in which God, "in the beginning," was dependent on existing matter. A further problem was the Gnostic belief, prevalent in the ancient world, that matter is the seedbed of evil. However, a solution to both problems was at hand—namely, *creatio ex nihilo*—the innovative doctrine that God created the world from absolute nothing. First of all, *creatio ex nihilo* shored up God's aseity and affirmed the essential goodness of creation. But further implications followed, and they led to a new understanding of God's relation to the world.

The theological turn to *creatio ex nihilo* placed creation in a new light. It meant that creation was not an event that happened once upon a time. As Augustine would say in the fourth century CE, it meant that time itself was created along with the world.[9] The upshot of this view is that God continues to be creative in the flow of present time and will continue to be creative in the future. Creation is nearby right now, and the passing of time is infused with significance. With this change in the status of time, creation becomes a veritable symbol, and it has the capacity to evoke awe and wonder that our world exists at all. The world did not have to be here. As theologian Brian Robinette puts it in *The Difference Nothing Makes*, the notion of creation from nothing "opens up human understanding of the utter gratuity of creation."[10]

Philosophy and science have also grappled with the problem of how everything came to be, though they use different terminology and proceed within different conceptual frameworks. In philosophy, a range of positions have appeared, from Gottfried

---

9. In chapter 14 of *The Confessions*, Augustine addresses God: "At no time, therefore, did you do nothing, since you had made time itself" (287).

10. Robinette, *Difference Nothing Makes*, 10.

Chapter Five: Kairos Calling

Leibnitz's earnest query, "Why is there something instead of nothing?" to Bertrand Russell's curt dismissal: "I should say that the universe is just here, and that is all."[11] In science, the dominant attitude has been to take existence at face value. Briefly stated, the universe has always been around. Classic physics told us so. But with Einstein's 1917 theory of relativity, everything—literally— became problematic. When Father Georges Lemaitre, in 1927, worked Einstein's discoveries into a model of spacetime, he showed that the universe must be either expanding or contracting. More surprising yet, Lemaitre's model showed that the entire universe must have originated from a single primeval point. Empirical observations from the Hubble telescope soon confirmed that galaxies around us are moving away from our own. Research over the past few decades has led to widespread agreement among physicists that the universe began with the so-called Big Bang approximately 13.8 billion years ago.

With the advent of the Big Bang cosmogony, reactions reverberated in the realm of religion. Theists were happy because now they could argue that the Big Bang hypothesis provided scientific backup for the biblical account of creation. And in 1951, Pope Pius XII proclaimed that the Big Bang proved that "creation took place in time, therefore there is a creator, [and] therefore God exists."[12] But atheists pulled the rug out from under these tidings when quantum mechanics rose to the forefront in physics. For from the quantum perspective, the scenario of all matter beginning from a single point is erroneous. As Jim Holt points out in his study, *Why Does the World Exist?*, quantum mechanics "opened up the conceptual possibility that the seed of the universe might have come into being without a cause, supernatural or otherwise. . . ."[13] From the perspective of quantum field theory, the universe began as a fluctuation in an unstable vacuum. Out of that "false" vacuum,

---

11. Leibniz and Russell quoted in Holt, *Why Does the World Exist*, 20 and 25. I am indebted to Holt's cogent (and surprisingly humorous) account of these developments in philosophy and in physics.

12. Quoted in Holt, *Why Does the World Exist*, 26.

13. Holt, *Why Does the World Exist*, 27.

particles "tunneled into existence out of nothingness."[14] Perhaps this notion of "quantum tunneling" in physics can no more be understood by lay persons than nonreligious persons can be cajoled into making sense of the Trinity. In any case, the notion has led to an array of standpoints. For example, the physicist Lawrence Krauss has focused on quantum tunneling in propounding his militant atheism. He elaborates his claims in a work with a telling title: *A Universe from Nothing*. However, as Holt points out, Krauss's position is not really a cosmogonic game changer. While the "nothing" of which Krauss speaks may be devoid of space, it is not nothingness in the absolute or existential sense. In other words, the quantum vacuum that Krauss calls "nothing" is highly structured. It's a soup of probabilities and fluctuating wave functions that obey "deep and complex laws of physics."[15] As with the primeval waters in Genesis, we are left asking, how did those quantum laws get there?

The puzzle of the creation of existence abides. Internecine disputes between astrophysicists shall go on. Theoretical shifts and new calculations will bring forth new paradigms. For example, in 2023 the newly deployed James Webb Space Telescope sighted "young" galaxies beyond limits previously imagined, thereby changing the estimated life of the universe from 13.8 billion to a mind-boggling 24 billion years. Go figure. At the same time, theists will continue to depict God as a personage behind it all, that is, as *a being* who used subatomic particles and nascent forces to kick-start creation. Atheists will refute these creationist scenarios, and the contestations will resume. But I think the door will remain open to contemplation of the mystery of creation as incalculable and as a symbol. Acknowledging that our finite minds can't solve it, apophatic discernment can invite "a patient discovery of the 'nothingness' from which we subsist."[16] We may find new ways of

14. Holt, *Why Does the World Exist*, 128.

15. Holt, *Why Does the World Exist*, 128. The same point—that is, that Krauss's "nothing" is not really nothing—is made by Susan Hossenfelder, *Existential Physics*, 32.

16. Robinette, *Difference Nothing Makes*, xvi.

Chapter Five: Kairos Calling

expressing sacramental wonder and more humane ways of living in the face of this original blessing.

Astonishment at creation is not a side effect of belief. Nor do we arrive at it as sure knowledge—at least not *controlling* knowledge. In chapter 2, controlling knowledge was defined as the coming together of a subject (a person) and object for the sake of control of the object by the subject. Clearly, creation is not a thing to be measured and put to practical use. Receiving knowledge, on the other hand, that is, the coming together of subject and object for the sake of *meaning*, can draw us closer to the mystery of creation, but again with the proviso that creation can never be merely an object. The apt approach is prayer, more specifically apophatic prayer, which is rooted in silence. Apophatic prayer, the practice of many mystics throughout Western history, can be distinguished from cataphatic prayer, which employs words to articulate the desire for intercession, confession, and thanksgiving. To enter quietly into silence, by contrast, is to acknowledge that the mystery of God's creation is beyond words, thoughts, and emotions. If we cannot fully apprehend God as the ground and abyss of being, we can experience God in *relation* to us, and the first language of that relation is silence.

Theologians such as Thomas Merton, Thomas Keating, Richard Rohr, and in an indirect way, Simone Weil, have inspired a contemporary spiritual movement to recover insights of the mystics and the practice of contemplative prayer. New translations of works by Meister Eckhart, Hildegard of Bingen, Marjorie Kempe, Marguerite Porete, Julian of Norwich, Teresa of Avila, John of the Cross, and the anonymous author of *The Cloud of Unknowing*, amongst others, attest to renewed awareness of the value of prayer that is centered in silence.[17] Many people experience centering prayer as liberating. It awakens a sense of life as a gift and of the human self as potentially free from the acquisitiveness of the imperial ego. And yet, contemplative prayer also awakens our awareness of

---

17. There are a number of works that explain and trace out the development of this spiritual movement, including Thomas Keating, *Invitation to Love* and Martin Laird, *Into the Silent Land*.

nothingness. If contemplative prayer is to be more than a trend, then, its practitioners can expect to become conversant with "the darkness of the lived moment."[18] To enter deep silence in apophatic prayer can be startling, for if calcified ideas about who we are fall away as we proceed, so do conventional notions about God. As Thomas Merton writes in *New Seeds of Contemplation*, "In the end the contemplative suffers the anguish of realizing that he *no longer knows what God is*. He may or may not mercifully realize that, after all, this is a great gain, because 'God is not a what,' not a 'thing.'"[19] We might add that the person making this great gain, who may or may not be "he," can begin to make historical connections. She may discover long-suppressed women mystics, such as Marguerite Porte, who, in the thirteenth century was well aware that God is no "thing." In *The Mirror of Simple Souls*, Porete states the crux of the matter: "God is none other than the One of whom one understands nothing perfectly . . . about whom one does not know how to say a word."[20]

CROSS

Along with creation, apophatic theology can expand our insights into Christianity's founding symbol. Perhaps more than any other facet of the Christian path, the symbol of the cross brings us face to face with the emptiness of loss. The shock of the crucifixion scene overturns human heroics. The ignoble end to the life of Jesus provides no uplifting call to revolutionary action. Moreover, the claim that the tortured and executed corpse of a suspected political criminal lies at the axis of the meaning of the Christian view of history presents an ongoing challenge to the triumphalist dogmas of the church. Gold-plated crucifixes escorting armies or decorating the palaces of authoritarian rulers do not fare well either.

18. Ernst Bloch uses this phrase to describe an aspect of the human condition. See Bloch, *Principle of Hope*, 12.

19. Merton, *New Seeds of Contemplation*, 13.

20. Quoted in Christie, *Insurmountable Darkness of Love*, 34. This passage is from Marguerite Porete, *Mirror of Simple Souls*, 102.

Chapter Five: Kairos Calling

Supernaturalist claims concerning the resurrection of Christ are also undermined. Honesty about the actuality of death is a precondition for experiencing the resurrection of Jesus as the Christ in its singular scope and power.

Apophatic theology is positioned to expose evasions of death. It hears a summons to look beneath the surface of everyday life to see what motivates people and what's really going on beneath cultural and ideological veils. For this task, theology is free to draw upon a host of writers, artists, and thinkers of various stripes who have made comparable observations. For example, we can listen to James Baldwin as he seeks to understand the mentality behind the racism that permeates American life. In *The Fire Next Time*, Baldwin notes that "most people guard and keep; they suppose that it is they themselves and what they identify with themselves that they are guarding and keeping, whereas what they are actually guarding and keeping is their system of reality and what they assume themselves to be."[21] What Baldwin calls "system of reality" could be defined as a person's belief system. I think what Baldwin is getting at here is that belief systems are always doing a great deal of work behind the scenes to provide people with "their sense of their own worth."[22] This need for self-esteem is incontrovertible. People will kill to keep it, especially when one's self-pleasing identity and the superiority of one's own group appear to be under threat. It is an incessant drive that leads Baldwin to wonder aloud about the tragic nature of life: "Perhaps the whole root of our trouble, the human trouble, is that we will sacrifice all the beauty of our lives, will imprison ourselves in totems, taboos, crosses, blood sacrifices, steeples, mosques, races, armies, flags, nations in order to deny the fact of death. . . ."[23] Baldwin knows that the dynamic fueling this "trouble" must be fully acknowledged if we hope "to build a better world—here there or anywhere."[24] Towards the end of *The Fire Next Time* he connects such hope with love: "I use the word 'love'

21. Baldwin, *Fire Next Time*, 86.
22. Baldwin, *Fire Next Time*, 76.
23. Baldwin, *Fire Next Time*, 91.
24. Baldwin, *Fire Next Time*, 103.

here not merely in the personal sense but as a state of being or a state of grace—not in the infantile American sense of being made happy but in the tough and universal sense of quest and daring and growth."[25]

Along with critiques like Baldwin's, research derived from multiple fields should inform apophatic theology. For example, consider the cultural anthropology of Ernest Becker and Rene Girard. Like Baldwin, Becker zeroed in on the human penchant for repressing mortality as the underlying source of so much "trouble." I have referred to Becker at several points in this study, especially in connecting fundamentalism and violence (chapter 4). Without repeating his theory, I want to note here that his extensive work on the destructive side of death denial did not lead him to resignation or despair. Like Baldwin, he recognized the tragedy of the human condition, yet Becker also aligned himself with the realistic hope born of open-minded religious faith. Readers of *The Denial of Death* are often surprised to learn that Becker was personally devout. He read the Psalms daily.[26] In those ancient texts, he would certainly have found corroborating words concerning human mortality. Psalm 103, for instance, speaks of fleeting human life in terms of dust and grass. But those words and images concerning death appear in the company and larger context of affirmations of the good of God's creation. Psalm 104 is a hymn to that elemental goodness. The point is that Becker does not take our essential creatureliness to be the problem in and of itself.[27] Unlike

25. Baldwin, *Fire Next Time*, 95.

26. Becker talks about his daily reading of the Psalms in "Letters from Ernest" collected by his friend, Harvey Bates, 217–27. When Sam Keen—in an interview with Becker when Becker was on his deathbed in 1973—noted the Stoic character of Becker's thought, Becker agreed, but added a qualification, namely, "the qualification that I believe in God." See Keen, "Conversation with Ernest Becker," 225. Science writer Brian Greene also notes Becker's religious side in *Until the End of Time*, 75. Lest anyone think that Becker's focus on death left him morbid, the contrary is true. On a personal note, I can report that when I was a graduate student at Simon Fraser University in Burnaby, Canada, the institution where Becker last taught, several of his former colleagues recalled his capacity for humor and laughter.

27. Though Becker did not discuss human finitude in systematic philo-

Chapter Five: Kairos Calling

the transhumanists of today who view mortality as a defect, albeit one that can be overcome through advancements in technology, Becker does not resent our finitude. He does not see it as a design flaw or as an ontological affront. For Becker, the cascading destruction wrought by humans stems from the attempt to keep the anxiety of non-being at bay. Like Baldwin, he thinks we could live differently. At a surprising point in his final work, *Escape from Evil*, Becker ponders the possibility of "living in primary awe" at the "miraculousness of creation."[28] Like many commentators who try to envision a relationship to existence that is not closed or fear-stricken, Becker mentions St. Francis of Assisi as someone who seemed to live in sacred fellowship with nature, finding awe and wonder in all living things.

Rene Girard (1923–2015) is another cultural critic who has much to offer apophatic theology. As with Becker, his interdisciplinary approach to human behavior has led to vital insights into the motives behind human violence. Perhaps even more than with Becker, Girard's insights disclose new levels of understanding in our interpretation of the Christian symbol of the cross.

Girard's breakthrough book, *Violence and the Sacred*, appeared in 1979. It surprised many scholars who assumed his interests were confined to literary study. Girard had become known in academic circles for his book, *Deceit, Desire, and the Novel* (1966), which focused on nineteenth-century novels. That he had bigger fish to fry, however, became apparent when he broadened his literary investigations to include Shakespearean drama, Greek tragedy, traditional mythology, and the Bible. His research expanded further when he incorporated anthropological data into his analyses

---

sophical terms, I think his approach accords with Paul Ricouer's affirmation of the ontology of finitude within the context of creation. See Aspray, *Ricœur at the Limits of Philosophy*, 3. Tillich makes a comparable claim: "The structure of finitude is good in itself, but under the conditions of estrangement it becomes a structure of destruction." See *Systematic Theology*, 2:71.

28. Becker, *Escape from Evil*, 163–64.

of human conflict as he found it articulated in literary classics. Out of this intellectual labor, Girard developed a full-fledged theory of human desire.

The key point in Girard's theory is that desire functions imitatively, or *mimetically*. Desire does not arise spontaneously as a by-product of individuality, a counterintuitive claim at odds with our sense of our own uniqueness. Rather, our desires are borrowed from others as we grow up. Beyond the most rudimentary food, clothing, and shelter that enable bodily survival, what we long for is shaped by the desires we see in others and in the culture at large. This copying is not straight-forwardly conscious and it does not unfold in a linear fashion; rather, it is socially mediated through triangulated interactions.[29]

In claiming that our desires are not our own, Girard also draws upon ontology. At the deepest level, he connects mimesis to a feeling of existential lack. In *Violence and the Sacred*, Girard notes that a person "desires *being*, something he himself lacks which some other person seems to possess. The subject thus looks to that other person to inform him of what he should desire in order to acquire that being. If the model, who is already endowed with superior being, desires some object, that object must surely be capable of conferring an even greater plentitude of being."[30] Framed in these terms, I think Girard's point is comparable to Kierkegaard's analysis of conformity as stemming from a person's missing subjectivity (chapter 4). Kierkegaard would agree with Girard that our longings have existential roots. Our desire for fullness of being also fits with Becker's insight that we strive to latch on to powers of being that serve as hedges against the threat of non-being.

Returning to Girard's theory, mimetic desire has a good side. Looking at others to pattern ourselves aids in identity formation and social learning. It fosters norms and high degrees of cooperation. However, the desires we appropriate from others who model them also make those others potential rivals. When we desire an

---

29. For a diagram depicting the transmission of mimetic desire, see Robinette, *Difference Nothing Makes*, 94–95.

30. Girard, *Violence and the Sacred*, 145–46.

Chapter Five: Kairos Calling

object, not for its inherent qualities, but just because others desire it, then the dark side of mimeticism rears its head. Yet it's not only objects that are held in contention; envy springs up around less tangible attributes like status and prestige. Rivalry then generates social conditions laden with the potential for violent escalation. And then all hell breaks loose, especially in situations aggravated by famine, epidemics, and war. Mimetic rivalry snowballs into reciprocal killing, a "contagion" that begins to tear the community asunder.

Violence escalates until a scapegoat is found to alleviate the crisis. This is the linchpin of Girard's theory: the mimetic crisis comes under control when hostility converges onto a despised person (or a small group). The war of all against all turns into the war of all against one—and it works. By providing the means for split factions to stand together, the destruction of the scapegoat has a pacifying effect. As factions come together and kill the persecuted one, the community finds catharsis and the stage is set for new social unanimity.

I am discussing Girard's theory in an abbreviated form here in order to cut to the theological chase. There are many other facets to his theory that could be noted, including the process by which the scapegoat grows to be venerated as sacred within the mythology of the murdering—now pacified—group. This phenomenon is noted in Girard's *Things Hidden Since the Foundation of the World* (1978), a book which once again took the academic world by surprise. The surprise was not Girard's focus on the Bible, but his claim that the Bible tells the story of mimetic violence from the point of view of the victims. Concern for the victim appears in Hebrew scripture, as in the stories of Abel and Joseph in Genesis and the Suffering Servant in Isaiah, but most thoroughly, according to Girard, in the gospel renderings of the crucifixion of Jesus. Christ, Girard argues, unmasks the scapegoating mechanism by unmistakably demonstrating that the victim of communal murder is innocent. Sacrificial violence is of human origin; it is not a divinely sanctioned restoration of order. The Hebrew prophetic tradition, to which Jesus belonged, had revealed *injustice* to be of human origin. In a parallel way, in the crucifixion of Jesus, we see that the victim is innocent, and that the injustice of violence stems from human collective action, not from God.

Girard's interpretation of the Gospels repudiates the conventional Christian idea of penal substitutionary atonement.[31] Elaborated by the Benedictine Monk Anselm (1033–1109), penal substitution holds that Jesus saves humanity through his death on the cross. The obedient death of Jesus was the ransom required by God the Father as the price or redemption of sinful humankind. But Girard sees this doctrine as a vestige of the mentality of sacrificial violence and, hence, a dangerous misreading of Jesus that runs across centuries. Girard's standpoint, summarily stated, is that "Jesus is killed not because God willed it, but because human beings wanted it."[32] Jesus died in solidarity with victims of mobs, and his death was meant to end the practice of sacrifice altogether.

For the early Christian communities, Jesus, a crucified criminal, was the Messiah whose death was followed by his rising up from the dead. The metaphor of rising to new life was not new. It had been used in later Judaism in relation to the fate of the Jewish martyrs of the Maccabean Revolt (167–160 BCE). Applied to Jesus, it took on a host of ramifications. Whether it was perceived in terms of visions and post-resurrection appearances or received in more symbolic terms, it changed everything. Above all, it was the ecstatic experience that Rome had not defeated Jesus when they crucified him, and that his followers could experience him after his death as a figure of the present. An event that had seemed to end in powerlessness on the cross had been transfigured while accruing ontological torque, so to speak. At least, that's the way Paul framed the matter in a letter to Christians in Corinth. From now on, he said, "If anyone is in Christ, there is a new creation" (2 Cor 5:17). A new reality had come into being. Was the end of sacrificial violence part of it?

---

31. For my understanding of Girard's theory of mimetic violence, I am indebted to Heim, *Saved from Sacrifice*.

32. Haven, *Evolution of Desire*, 183.

Chapter Five: Kairos Calling

Over time, the resurrection event has generated divergent interpretations. I can't hope to parse those many views here, but I think it's important simply to note that the fundamentalist view—that is, that the body of Jesus was literally resuscitated and supernaturally transmogrified—is not the only one, even though many religious and anti-religious people alike seem to assume as much. Today, nonliteralist interpretations are open to more capacious understandings of the meaning of the Easter story. For example, Barbara Brown Taylor points out that "Christ's gift to humankind . . . is not about paying debt but about showing what divine life and death look like in the flesh."[33] John Dominic Crossan has argued that resurrection does not simply concern the solitary Christ figure. Western Christianity has lost the awareness of resurrection as a *collective* rising to new life. According to Crossan, the iconography in Eastern Christianity has rightly maintained that the resurrection discloses the presence of God acting in history as it becomes visible in the entire community of faith.[34]

Girard's research into the origins and history of mimetic conflict affected him personally. In particular, his work on Dostoevsky and the Bible led him to see the demonic reach of toxic violence in shaping human behavior. In his book, *When These Things Begin* (2014), he states his recognition starkly: "More than ever, I am convinced that history has meaning, and that meaning is terrifying."[35] Cynthia Haven, Girard's biographer, has traced out the shift in his beliefs as they changed from atheist to agnostic to the standpoint of a questioning Christian. Girard's spiritual journey has perturbed scholars who take it as axiomatic that religion is a thing of the past. But Girard's insights have opened doors in theology and in the humanities, despite rivalry of the academic kind. His thinking moved in a Christian direction because he couldn't shake the sense that we are in an existential emergency. He saw a pressing need to imitate Christ's renunciation of violence. As

---

33. Taylor, "At Home With Strangers," 34.
34. Crossan and Crossan, *Resurrecting Easter*, 45–59.
35. Girard, *When These Things Begin*, 129.

Haven notes, he "increasingly turned to the theme of 'forgiveness'" as "a key to breaking the cycles of vengeance."[36]

Before leaving Girard and Becker, the connections between their work and science should be noted. The anti-science declarations of Christian nationalists and fundamentalists around the globe convince many people that religion and science are inherently opposed. But that view is disproven when it comes to Becker and Girard. Social science experiments and brain research backing up their theories show how cross-fertilization between science and religion happens.

In the case of Becker, the development of Terror Management Theory (beginning in 1986) has generated hundreds of empirical studies demonstrating the role of the fear of death in human activity.[37] Experiments conducted around the world have demonstrated how awareness of death can trigger worldview defenses and hostile attitudes to other races, religions, and nations. The *cross-cultural* aspect of these studies is striking. On an everyday scale, the experiments show how the creation and maintenance of cultural worldviews provide persons with symbolic structures for achieving self-esteem. Self-esteem in turn provides a buffering function that enables persons to cope with the debilitating anxiety that one day we will decay and die. But awareness of these deep psychological processes need not end there. Is there a way in which advancements in our understanding of death anxiety might lead us to live together more peacefully? The Ernest Becker Foundation answers "yes." As an organization first launched in 1993 to make the works of Ernest Becker better known, it has become a nexus for scholars and lay persons worldwide who recognize how deeply our own

---

36. Haven, *Evolution of Desire*, 278. Though Hannah Arendt was writing from very different political assumptions and undertook different kinds of analyses from Girard, it is striking that she concluded that "the discoverer of the role of forgiveness in the realm of human affairs was Jesus of Nazareth." See *Human Condition*, 239n76.

37. See Solomon et al., *Worm at the Core*. This foundational text in Terror Management Theory reviews a large body of research supporting Ernest Becker's claim that "mortality salience" engenders many forms of societal behavior, including flagrant scapegoating.

Chapter Five: Kairos Calling

mortality affects human behavior and psychology. Through public education and workshops based on Terror Management Theory, the Ernest Becker Foundation is now a resource for people who believe that "the more aware we are of our own response patterns, the more we can make better choices and live more easily with one another."[38]

In the case of Girard, scientific support for mimetic theory came in the mid-1990s with a neurological discovery. Studies of the development of newborns and infants had led to the detection of *mirror neurons*, a system in the brain that is activated by the perception of goal-directed action in others. You don't have to go to a laboratory to research this phenomenon; you can simply observe that newborns put out their tongues to imitate adults from the natal get go, prior to developing other brain processes like using language. The implication is that if mirror neurons endow humans with the ability to copy, they may well form the neurological basis for mimetic desire and our ability to understand the actions of others. Andrew Meltzoff, who has led many of these studies, puts it concisely: "We're a role model for babies from the moment they look up at us and begin to sculpt their own activities according to what they see in the culture around them."[39] If imitation is central to the development of much societal behavior—actions that can be both positive and negative, as Girard repeatedly points out—further study of mirror neurons could increase knowledge on several fronts. For example, such research could illuminate how the conduct of people changes for the worse when they are in crowds. In a more positive vein, such research has initiated educational practices aimed at enhancing the desire and capacity for empathy.

The insights of Becker and Girard should inform theology. When theology attempts to grasp the darkness and loss in our lives, it can learn from their excavations beneath the norms of culture and the self-deceptions of the human soul. Becker and

---

38. "Mortality Awareness Preparedness Project," *The Ernest Becker Foundation*, Seattle, Washington, October 13, 2023, www.ernestbecker.org.

39. Quoted in Haven, *Evolution of Desire*, 220. See also Garrels, *Mimesis and Science*.

Girard also expose the deeper strata of religion in ways that give rise to questions theology must ask again and again. For example, what makes religion creative in one era and then turn on a dime to become destructive in another? A case in point: the crucifixion of Jesus may have deconstructed the scapegoat mechanism—and subverted vicarious atonement in the process—but that did not stop self-proclaimed followers of Jesus from creating scapegoats in subsequent generations. As James Carroll points out, "In preaching the good news that the innocent victim Jesus had brought an end to scapegoating by showing scapegoating for what it was, His followers scapegoated. Under pressures generated by the Roman wars, these members of Jesus' own people scapegoated other members of Jesus' own people."[40] Historians of the ancient world often tie this turnaround to Constantine's conversion to Christianity in 313 CE, for by subsequently establishing Christianity as the official religion of the Roman Empire he changed the path of this new religion from a prophetic movement against imperialism to one that became dominated by it. Turning to the medieval world, we find the scapegoating mentality alive and well in the Crusaders attack on Jerusalem in 1099, when Christian armies mercilessly slaughtered all the Muslims and Jews of that city. As the modern world arose out of the medieval context, the domination politics of empire became a pervasive ideology, nowhere more apparent than in the so-called Doctrine of Discovery—the legitimizing laws that Christian European monarchies deployed, under the guise of discovering new land, to seize resources and the lands inhabited by indigenous peoples. For millions of people in the "new world" who were enslaved, or displaced, or liquidated during this extended tragedy, the cross represented aggression and racism. Many would have looked upon the cross as we view the swastika today. This historical reality is studiously ignored nowadays by Christian Nationalists who, ever enamored by the image of the lone cowboy with a gun, wish to restore the mindset of Manifest Destiny.

---

40. Carroll, *Truth at the Heart of the Lie*, 259.

CHAPTER FIVE: KAIROS CALLING

Here is another historical reality: while often few in number, there are those who see injustice and resist it.[41] There are people like Bartolomé de las Casas (1484–1566), for instance, who recognized in the life of Christ a vision of love and compassion. A contemporary of Christopher Columbus, las Casas found the courage to stand against the mass murder and abuse of Indians by the conquistadores. When he became a clergyman, he began a campaign to stop ongoing genocide during Spain's conquest of the Americas. As a witness and activist, he spent fifty years documenting atrocities, fighting slavery, and consistently siding with Native Americans against the colonizers. Las Casas did not take this position as a career move; his commitment stemmed from a calling that he declared clearly in his defense: "From Christ, the eternal truth, we have the commandment 'You must love your neighbor as yourself.'"[42]

LOVE WAS HIS MEANING

In these words, uttered centuries ago, las Casas based his life on love and the demand it calls forth. Yet this is not an abstract sense of love conceived as a cosmic principle. I do not wish to devalue the level at which love may be understood philosophically as, say, the attraction of all things to all things. According to the first letter of John, "God is love" (1 John 4:16). But the concrete nature of love becomes visible in human experience. When God is seen as acting continuously within natural and historical processes, then we can discern how humans can participate with God as the underlying force of love in the world. As Diana Butler Bass points out in *A People's History of Christianity*, followers of the Jesus path discover love above all in the life of Christ, for "love is what he preached

---

41. For a film portrayal of a twentieth-century example of resistance to injustice see Terrence Malick's *A Hidden Life* (2019) based on the life of Franz Jägerstätter. He was executed for refusing to back down from his stance against Nazi fascism.

42. Quoted in Osborn, *Humanism, and the Death of God*, 97.

and what he embodied."[43] Another symbol of this embodiment—a symbol that expands our understanding beyond fixation on the cross—is the banquet table. For a crucial part of the social action of Jesus was eating with those who were oppressed by or excluded from the dominant purity system and temple structures. When he was not judged for eating too much (Luke 7:34), Jesus was attacked for eating with "tax collectors" and designated "sinners" (Matt 9:10–11), not to mention lepers, as Mark's Gospel tells us (Mark 14:3). In short, the table fellowship of Jesus discloses unconditional love already present in the world.

Unconditional love cannot be managed. Its presence and appearances are not subject to control. Hence, when it comes to theological talk about God's love, the apophatic proclivity for giving the negative its due should be on task. It should point out that those who have been grasped by Jesus's love and ministry cannot lord it over others with the claim that they have matched his message to their formulations and stagings. Turning to the academic world, we should be aware that scholars of the New Testament era cannot shoehorn understanding of the impact of Jesus into the historical terms of cause and effect. In another scholarly vein, for all the insights that can be gleaned from René Girard, the life and ministry of Jesus can't entirely be explained as performing an anthropological function. In our personal lives, we may come to know love is more than justice and greater than faith and hope, but that doesn't place love at our spiritualizing disposal. The astonishing experience that love is stronger than death and liberating in ways we never thought possible doesn't remove the injustice, evil, and tragedy endured by generations in the past.

Returning to the terms of chapter 2, to say that love cannot be calculated means that it is best understood in terms of receiving knowledge. That is, the scope and value of sacred love cannot be known and demonstrated *objectively*, but its meaning can be received *experientially*. We can see an example of such reception in the life of the fourteenth-century English laywoman, Julian of Norwich. In her adult life she barely survived a life-threatening

---

43. Bass, *People's History of Christianity*, 31.

illness. What's more, she lived in a time and place decimated by famine, epidemic violence, and recurring waves of the black plague. One commentator describes her life and times as "terrifyingly precarious."[44] Yet in spite of such danger and sorrow, we find her speaking of the imminent wellness of all things in God's creation. In *Revelations of Divine Love*, she recounts her vision of Christ as our unconditionally loving mother. When she summarizes her teachings at the end of this book, she shares precious words with her reader: "Would you like to know our Lord's meaning in all this? Know it well: love was his meaning."[45] To embrace such an answer is no doubt a personal event, but this knowledge is not merely subjective. In Kierkegaard's terms, the meaning of love, when it arrives for those who are open to receive it, is necessarily *mediated* through our subjectivity. Whether in Julian's day or our own, it is still the kind of knowledge that changes our relationships to ourselves, to others, and to the world.

Speaking of Kierkegaard, I wish to close this chapter by noting an incident from his life. As mentioned in chapter 4, Kierkegaard's short life was marked by detrimental factors stemming from his overbearing father and highly dysfunctional family. The deaths of siblings, his physical oddities, and his melancholia also figured into the aberrant environment in which he grew up. Nevertheless, at age twenty-seven we find him finishing his university studies, dazzling many with his intellect, and engaged to a bright and beautiful woman named Regine Olsen. The happy courtship lasted thirteen months. Then Kierkegaard abruptly ended it in a heartless fashion. The aftermath left Regine devastated, her family humiliated, and Kierkegaard ensconced in a round of rationalizations that would pervade his thinking for the rest of his life. To read Kierkegaard today is to recognize his obsession with Regine lingering in many of his themes, and, in short, to realize that he never stopped loving her. Why had he broken off the engagement? Kierkegaard's reasons range from reticence about marriage, to his

---

44. Farley, *Thirst of God*, 46. I am indebted to Wendy Farley's rich discussion of Julian of Norwich.

45. Julian of Norwich, *Showings*, 224.

concern that his chronic melancholia would be debilitating for Regine, to a belief that his singular religious calling meant he was destined to be excluded from normal family life.

To follow, over the course of their lives, the ruminations of Soren (in his pages and pages of journals) and Regine's conflicted thoughts (in her letters to others) is to be reminded repeatedly of the behavioral constraints of middle-class life in nineteenth-century Copenhagen, when a glance in the street or a nod in church could mean everything.[46] Still, when Regine married and was ready to leave Copenhagen, now as Regine Schlegel, she went to find him. She had already forgiven him long ago, and, in my opinion, she had never stopped loving him for who he was. Her concern for him led her to forget about the constraints and search for him in the streets of the city, where he was surely to be found, as usual, acting out his Socratic fantasies. She approached him. It surprised him. She said simply, "God bless you—may all go well with you." Kierkegaard published thirty-eight books over the course of his life, including an especially remarkable one titled *Works of Love*, yet there is something in Regine's gesture on that day that is every bit as revealing as anything he ever wrote. That is what love is like. It finds you.

---

46. This last encounter between Kierkegaard and Regina Schlegel (née Olsen) is recounted by Backhouse, *Kierkegaard*, 180. Also see Garff, *Kierkegaard's Muse*.

Conclusion

I'm going to go out on a limb here and assert that we all have to die.
—Scott Samuelson[1]

In a dark time, the eye begins to see. —Theodore Roethke[2]

"WE FORGOT THAT WE are finite, and we forgot the abyss of nothingness surrounding us"—these words are from a sermon delivered by Paul Tillich at Union Theological Seminary in the middle of the twentieth century. He is referring to the terrible awakening that came with World War I when European civilization, under the illusion that it was the culmination of a great era of progress, entered into four years of mechanized slaughter. Tillich himself was under that illusion when he set off to serve as a chaplain on the front lines. He was part of a generation that took pride in patriotic duty and was filled with conventional optimism about advancing human knowledge. As Tillich puts it, his generation had successfully kept "the lid" on death, but "suddenly the lid was torn off." They became "the generation of world wars, revolutions, and mass migrations," and above all, a generation who "rediscovered the reality of death."[3]

We again want to forget the abyss of nothingness that surrounds us. We have updated the ways of keeping nothingness at

1. Samuelson, *Seven Ways of Looking at Pointless Suffering*, 159.
2. Roethke, *Collected Poems*, 116.
3. Tillich, "Love Is Stronger Than Death," 170–71.

bay. To say as much is not to shrink from our capacity to affirm life. To reflect on human transience and precarity is not to block out the joy, humor, and delight that suffuse life. The point of remembering human limits is to recognize that many of our buffers against nothingness are false. When the falseness is exposed and the proverbial lid comes off, we encounter forms of overwhelming destruction. You can call that destruction evil or the manifestation of the demonic, but it is not supernatural. It is the power of the negation of being that derives its power from the being it negates. Stated another way, where the power for good increases, the power for evil increases as well. Where does meaning then reside?

When our situation is put in ontological and existential terms, it can sound merely abstract. At various points in this study, I have weighed using more figurative expressions in place of such discourse. For example, when the poet, Forrest Gander, speaks of "a loss that every other loss fits inside,"[4] I wonder if he has found the best way of capturing what we feel when we encounter non-being. Or in order to refer to "the human condition," there are moments when I think it might be better to let Samuel Beckett's character, Hamm, say it: "You're on earth: there's no cure for that!"[5] On the other hand, abstract language has its uses too. For example, ontological terms enable us to traverse the planet and appreciate how very different cultures use different names to express similar spiritual truths. The relationship between humans and gods is one of them. If we understand the names of divinities as signifying *powers of being*, for instance, we can see an array of imaginative cultural expression, instead of cartoon-like characters tied to moribund plots. When it comes to the term *being*, our understanding is broadened when we recognize how, say, the Vedanta tradition in India wrestled with this notion. A further example from the ancient world is Parmenides's remarkable breakthrough to the thought of being within the milieu of pre-Socratic philosophy.

With a caveat concerning the limits of ontological language in play, then, the main points in this study can be summarized as

4. Gander, *Be With*, 27.
5. Beckett, *Endgame*, 37.

CONCLUSION

follows. The starting point and touchstone throughout is the fact of human finitude. We live out our days adjacent to non-being. To help us grasp this reality, we can draw upon the apophatic orientation in theology, an outlier to the dominant modes of thought today.[6] From this angle of vision, we can begin to see and to acknowledge pervasive absence. In giving non-being due recognition, many of the "givens" of human life are unsettled. We also come to see how the apophatic standpoint can be expanded conceptually. Once again, the starting point is the recognition of illusions around human endeavors that stem from our denial of death. On that basis, apophatic thinking provides a warrant for radical critique—in particular, for questioning the false security of both authoritarian religion and self-sufficient secularism. Finally, the apophatic path provides a way of deepening our relationship with the God beyond God, the God who is not *a* supreme being but the unconditional "ground" of being and nothingness. This God is not a person, but not less than a person.[7] As Anne Lamott puts it, this God is "way beyond us, and deep inside."[8] This God appears when meaninglessness is overturned. As living spirit, this God can be experienced everywhere renewing creation, healing individuals, and bringing freedom and justice to exploited communities.

Apophatic insight undercuts the longing for immortality and the projection of immortality onto culture heroes. For example, John Dominic Crossan brings such insight to his book, *Jesus: A Revolutionary Biography*. Crossan first notes that the crucifixion of Jesus was, amongst other things, a brutal political execution in an ancient police state. He then points to archeological evidence

---

6. In modern academia, theology has been increasingly ignored or outrightly dismissed as inconsequential (or simply embarrassing). Within the world of theology itself, there have long been spiritual schools and movements outside or at odds with the church, including the Desert Fathers and Mothers, the Beguine movement, and Celtic Christianity.

7. I first encountered this idea in Thich Nhat Hanh's book *Going Home: Jesus and Buddha as Brothers*, 12. Thich Nhat Hanh attributes the notion that God "is not less than a person" to a "German theologian," who turns out to be Paul Tillich.

8. Lamott, *Help, Thanks, Wow*, 7.

that suggests, under these conditions, the body of Jesus, following crucifixion, would likely have been left to be eaten by wild dogs.[9] This account may be an affront to belief that Jesus was supernaturally resuscitated. On the other hand, in what one might call an act of apophatic courage, Crossan opens up an understanding of resurrection that refuses to be confined by the dictates of biblical literalism.

In its capacity for critique, the apophatic standpoint is well placed to question the limits of triumphalist religion. When religions congeal into staid systems of belief touting immaculate answers that vanquish all questions, doubt is anesthetized. But how can you appreciate the answers and make them your own if you have never seriously asked the questions? Nathaniel Hawthorne's well-known observation about Herman Melville—he "can neither believe nor be comfortable in his unbelief; and he is too honest and courageous not to try to do one or the other"[10]—describes a state of concern that is closer to faith than any declaration of creedal adherence. Particularly in the case of theistic religions, when the act of confessing becomes formulaic, perhaps the apophatic thing to do is to side with Meister Eckhart and pray to God "to rid us of 'God.'"

An apophatic standpoint can also criticize secularism. In the name of human progress and reason, secularism rightly attacks irrational and destructive forms of religion. In the process, though, it often depends on reason with an instrumental bent. That is, it deploys a kind of analysis that presumes everything can be made into an object of calculation and control. This kind of reason is the source of the immense and incessant technological innovation driving our capitalist consumer culture today. However, it is also at the root of the malaise of modernity in its disassociation from questions of meaning and from a range of human experience

---

9. Crossan, *Jesus*, 126 and 154. This point is also made by James P. Carse: "What is often overlooked is that in the gospel account Jesus dies a real death. . . . But the habit of Christians to interpret the [resurrection] event as a guarantee of immortality has no basis in the New Testament," See *Religious Case Against Belief*, 170–71.

10. Hawthorne, *English Notebooks*, 433.

Conclusion

that cannot be efficiently translated into commodified terms. One experience that runs counter to such malaise is the sense of life as uncalculated grace. It begins in awe that life is here at all. It grows into the realization that we are in kinship with all life. But you can't measure or encode this realization. It doesn't boost productivity. The sense of life as a gift resists reification. Yet it is not at odds with scientific facts. For example, science has determined that life began on our planet approximately 3.7 billion years ago. Fundamentalists do not want to know this fact, so they suppress it. But religious persons who are not fundamentalists can grasp this fact, respect the reasoning behind it, and then supplement it with a kind of knowing that is different from explanation. A further fact, namely, that life on earth has gone through five mass extinctions over the course of evolution, makes room for further reflection, which may include apprehension at our transitoriness, ponderings of our purpose as self-conscious life, and consciousness of wonder at our profound relationship to the earth.

Throughout this study, I have referred to literary works as conveying truths inaccessible to instrumental reason. Musical works could be cited just as readily for their capacity to point to the ineffable. As George Steiner says, music "puts our being as men and women in touch with that which transcends the sayable, which outstrips the analyzable."[11] One contemporary composer who meets this calling is Arvo Pärt. In sacred instrumental and choral works, he seems to have consciously adopted, as one commentator notes, "an apophatic musical style."[12] That style stems from the silence featured in his minimalist compositions, but no less from the intimation of spiritual strength underneath the silence.

Apophatic works of all kinds can remind us, in Tillich's words, of "the nothingness surrounding us." They entail a reckoning with the darker side of life; they can also disclose an experience of renewal that opens on the other side of loss. The writings of Rainer Maria Rilke often reenact this double movement. For example, in *Sonnets to Orpheus*, he invokes the reader to "be—and at the same

---

11. Quoted in Brown and Hopps, *Extravagance of Music*, 3.
12. Brown and Hopps, *Extravagance of Music*, 9.

time know the implication / of non-being, the endless ground of your inner vibration, / so you can fulfill it fully just this once."[13] To affirm one's life in spite of mortality and in full awareness of non-being is the essential creative task. In a comparable way, author Mary Gordon relates creativity to the encounter with what she calls "the living darkness." She finds living darkness "at the center of the 'nothing' that [King] Lear learns about, the black of Mark Rothko's last panels, a black that contains in itself, invisible, the germs from which life can reknit itself and spring."[14]

I want to close here with Denise Levertov's way of expressing the experience of life "reknit." In her collection of verse, *Oblique Prayers*, she circumnavigates many emotions, including "happiness." Yet near the end of *Oblique Prayers*, in a poem titled "Of Being," she admits, "I know this happiness / is provisional." It is an acknowledgment that runs deep. This writer is aware that there are always "looming presences—/ great suffering, great fear." Even when those threats seem to disperse, she knows they have only withdrawn "into peripheral vision." Then, with no insulating illusions, and within the space that her reflections have opened, what matters most enters:

> but ineluctable this shimmering
> of wind in the blue leaves:
>
> this flood of stillness
> widening the lake of sky:
>
> this need to dance,
> this need to kneel:
>   this mystery:[15]

---

13. Rilke, *Duino Elegies and Sonnets to Orpheus*, 163.
14. Gordon, "Deadly Sins," 3.
15. Levertov, "Of Being," 734.

Bibliography

Arendt, Hannah. *The Human Condition*. Chicago: University of Chicago Press, 1958.
Aristotle. *Poetics*. Translated by James Hulton. New York: W. W. Norton, 1982.
Armstrong, Karen. *Fields of Blood: Religion and the History of Violence*. New York: Alfred A. Knopf, 2014.
Aroosi, Jamie. *The Dialectical Self: Kierkegaard, Marx, and the Making of the Modern Subject*. Philadelphia: University of Pennsylvania Press, 2019.
Aspray, Barnabas. *Ricoeur at the Limits of Philosophy: God, Creation, and Evil*. Cambridge: Cambridge University Press, 2022.
Augustine. *The Confessions of St. Augustine*. New York: Doubleday, 1960.
Baard, Rachel Sophia. *Sexism and Sin-Talk: Feminist Conversations on the Human Condition*. Louisville, KY: Westminster John Knox, 2019.
Backhouse, Stephen. *Kierkegaard: A Single Life*. Grand Rapids: Zondervan, 2016.
Baldwin, James. *The Fire Next Time*. New York: Vintage, 1993.
Bass, Diana Butler. *A People's History of Christianity: The Other Side of the Story*. New York: Harper One, 2010.
Bates, Harvey. "Letters from Ernest." *Christian Century* 94 (1977) 217–27.
Beal, Timothy. "The Bible Is Dead—Long Live the Bible." *The Chronicle of Higher Education* 57 (2011) B6-B8.
———. *When Time Is Short: Finding Our Way in the Anthropocene*. Boston: Beacon, 2022.
Beck, Richard. *The Slavery of Death*. Eugene, OR: Cascade, 2014.
Becker, Ernest. *The Denial of Death*. New York: Free Press, 1973.
———. *Escape from Evil*. New York: Free Press, 1975.
Beckett, Samuel. *Endgame*. London: Faber, 1976.
Biale, David. "Isaac Luria." *The Norton Anthology of World Religions: Judaism*. Edited by David Biale and Jack Miles. New York: W. W. Norton, 2015.
Biale, David, and Jack Miles, eds. *The Norton Anthology of World Religions: Judaism*. New York: W. W. Norton, 2015.
Blake, William. "Auguries of Innocence." In *Collected Poems*, edited by W. B. Yeats, 88–89. New York: Routledge, 2002.

BIBLIOGRAPHY

Bloch, Ernest. *The Principle of Hope*. Translated by Neville Plaice et al. Cambridge, MA: MIT Press, 1986.

Bolz-Weber, Nadia. *Shameless: A Sexual Reformation*. Colorado Springs, CO: Convergent, 2019.

Borg, Marcus. *Meeting Jesus Again for the First Time: The Historical Jesus at the Heart of Contemporary Faith*. New York: Harper One, 1995.

Borg, Marcus J., and John Dominic Crossan. *The First Paul: Reclaiming the Radical Visionary Behind the Church's Conservative Icon*. San Francisco: Harper One, 2010.

Brown, David, and Gavin Hopps. *The Extravagance of Music*. London: Palgrave Macmillan, 2018.

Brueggemann, Walter. *The Prophetic Imagination: 40th Anniversary Edition*. Minneapolis: Fortress, 2018.

Buber, Martin. *I and Thou*. Translation by Walter Kaufmann. New York: Charles Scribner's Sons, 1970.

Bukowski, Charles. *The Captain Is Out to Lunch and the Sailors Have Taken Over the Ship*. Illustrated by Robert Crumb. New York: Harper Collins, 1998.

Calvin, John. *Institutes of the Christian Religion* (1559), I.11.8. Edited by John T. McNeill. Translated by Ford Lewis. Philadelphia: Westminster, 1960.

Campbell, Joseph. *The Hero with a Thousand Faces*. Princeton: Princeton University Press: 1973.

———. *Myths to Live By*. New York: Penguin, 1972.

———. *Thou Art That: Transforming Religious Metaphor*. Los Angeles: Joseph Campbell Foundation, 2016.

Carroll, James. *The Truth at the Heart of the Lie: How the Catholic Church Lost Its Soul: A Memoir of Faith*. New York: Random House, 2021.

Carse, James P. *The Religious Case Against Belief*. New York: Penguin, 2008.

Case, Anne, and Angus Deaton. *Deaths of Despair, and the Future of Capitalism*. Princeton: Princeton University Press, 2020.

Champion, James. "The Parable as an Ancient and Modern Form." *Journal of Literature and Theology* 3 (1989) 16–39.

Chilton, Bruce. *The Herods: Murder, Politics, and the Art of Succession*. Minneapolis: Fortress, 2021.

Christie, Douglas E. *The Insurmountable Darkness of Love: Mysticism, Loss, and the Common Life*. New York: Oxford University Press, 2022.

Churchland, Patricia S. *The Computational Brain*. Cambridge, MA: MIT Press, 1992.

Clarke, Sathianathan. *Competing Fundamentalisms: Violent Extremism in Christianity, Islam, and Hinduism*. Louisville, KY: Westminster John Knox, 2017.

Cohen, Leonard. "Anthem." In *Stranger Music: Selected Poems and Songs*, 373–74. New York: Pantheon, 1993.

Coleridge, Samuel Taylor. *The Statesman's Manual*. Sydney: Wentworth, 2019.

BIBLIOGRAPHY

Crossan, John Dominic. *How to Read the Bible and Still Be a Christian*. New York: HarperCollins, 2015.
———. *Jesus: A Revolutionary Biography*. San Francisco: HarperSanFrancisco, 1994.
———. *The Power of Parable: How Fiction by Jesus Became Fiction About Jesus*. New York: HarperCollins, 2012.
———. *Render Unto Caeser: The Struggle Over Christ and Culture in the New Testament*. New York: Harper One, 2022.
———. *Who Is Jesus?* Louisville, KY: Westminster John Knox, 1996.
Crossan, John Dominic, and Sara Crossan. *Resurrecting Easter: How the West Lost and the East Kept the Original Easter Vision*. New York: Harper One, 2018.
Darwin, Charles. *The Autobiography of Charles Darwin*. Portland, OR: Floating, 2009.
Dickinson, Emily. *Final Harvest: Emily Dickinson's Poems*. New York: Little, Brown, 1964.
Dodd, C. H. *The Parables of the Kingdom*. Rev. ed. New York: Charles Scribner's Sons, 1961.
Dorrien, Gary. *In a Post-Hegelian Spirit*. Waco: Baylor University Press, 2020.
Dostoevsky, Fyodor. *The Brothers Karamazov*. Translated by Richard Pevear and Larissa Volokhonsky. San Francisco: North Point, 1990.
Dowling, David. *William Faulkner: Macmillan Modern Novelists*. New York: Palgrave Macmillan, 1989.
Eagleton, Terry. *Faith, Reason, and Revolution: Reflections on the God Debate*. New Haven: Yale University Press, 2010.
Eckhart, Meister. *Meister Eckhart: The Essential Sermons, Commentaries, Treaties and Defense*. Translated by Edmund College and Bernard McGinn. New York: Paulist, 1981.
———. *Meister Eckhart: An Introduction to the Study of His Works with an Anthology of His Sermons*. Edited and Translated by James M. Clark. New York: Thomas Nelson and Sons, 1957.
Einstein, Albert. *Living Philosophies*. New York: Simon and Schuster, 1931.
Eliade, Mircea. *The Quest: History and Meaning in Religion*. Chicago: University of Chicago Press, 1961.
Epicurus. "Letter to Menoeceus." In *The Art of Happiness*, translated by George K. Strodach, 156–57. New York: Penguin, 2012.
Farley, Wendy. *The Thirst of God: Contemplating God's Love with Three Women Mystics*. Louisville, KY: Westminster John Knox, 2015.
———. *Tragic Vision and Divine Compassion: A Contemporary Theodicy*. Louisville, KY: Westminster John Knox, 1990.
Faulkner, William. *Selected Letters of William Faulkner*. Edited by Joseph Blotner. New York: Random House, 1977.
Fowles, John. *The Magus*. Rev. ed. London: Random House, 1987.
Franke, William. *Apophatic Paths from Europe to China: Regions Without Borders*. New York: State University of New York Press, 1918.

Bibliography

———. *On What Cannot Be Said: Apophatic Discourses in Philosophy, Religion, Literature, and the Arts.* Vol. 1. Notre Dame: University of Notre Dame Press, 2007.

———. *Secular Scriptures.* Columbus: Ohio State University, 2016.

Frye, Northrop. *Collected Works,* Vol. 4. Toronto: University of Toronto Press, 1996–2011.

———. *The Educated Imagination.* Bloomington: Indiana University Press, 1964.

Gander, Forrest. *Be With.* New York: New Directions, 2018.

Garff, Joakim. *Kierkegaard's Muse: The Mystery of Regine Olsen.* Princeton: Princeton University Press, 2017.

Garrels, Scott, ed. *Mimesis and Science: Empirical Research on Imitation and the Mimetic Theory of Culture and Religion.* East Lansing: Michigan State University Press, 2011.

Gillespie, Michael Allen. *Nietzsche's Final Teaching.* Chicago: University of Chicago Press, 2017.

———. *The Theological Origins of Modernity.* Chicago: University of Chicago Press, 2008.

Girard, Rene. *Violence and the Sacred.* Translated by Patrick Gregory. Baltimore: Johns Hopkins University Press, 1977.

———. *When These Things Begin: Conversations with Michel Treguer.* Translated by Trevor Cribben. East Lansing: Michigan State University Press, 2014.

Gopnik, Blake. *Warhol.* New York: Harper Collins, 2020.

Gordon, Mary. "The Deadly Sins / Anger; The Fascination Begins in the Mouth." *New York Times,* June 13,1993. https://www.nytimes.com/1993/06/13/books/the-deadly-sins-anger-the-fascination-begins-in-the-mouth.html.

Greene, Brian. *Until the End of Time: Mind, Matter, and Our Search for Meaning in an Evolving Universe.* New York: Knopf, 2020.

Hanh, Thich Nhat. *Going Home: Jesus and Buddha as Brothers.* New York: Riverhead, 1990.

Hall, Douglas John. *The Cross in Our Context.* Minneapolis: Fortress, 2003.

Hall, Shannon. "Exxon Knew About Climate Change Almost 40 Years Ago." *Scientific American* 313 (October 26, 2015). https://www.scientificamerican.com/article/exxon-knew-about-climate-change-almost-40-years-ago/.

Hammarskjöld, Dag. *Markings.* New York: Alfred A. Knopf, 1965.

Harries, Richard. *The Beauty and the Horror.* London: SPCK, 2016.

Havel, Vaclav. *Letters to Olga.* New York: Knopf, 1988.

Haven, Cynthia L. *Evolution of Desire: A life of Rene Girard.* East Lansing: Michigan State University Press, 2018.

Hawthorne, Nathaniel. *The English Notebooks.* Edited by Randall Stewart. New York: Russell and Russell, 1962.

Hedges, Chris. *American Fascists: The Christian Right and the War on America.* New York: Free Press, 2006.

Hegel, Georg W. F. *The Philosophy of History.* Translated by J. Sibree. New York: Prometheus, 1991.

BIBLIOGRAPHY

Heim, S. Mark. *Saved from Sacrifice: A Theology of the Cross.* Grand Rapids: Eerdmans, 2006.

Heschel, Abraham J. *The Prophets.* New York: Harper Perennial, 2001.

Hesla, David. "Greek and Christian Tragedy: Notes Toward a Theology of Literary History." *Journal of the American Academy of Religion Thematic Studies* 49 (1981) 70–75.

Hodgson, Peter C. *Winds of the Spirit: A Constructive Christian Theology.* Louisville, KY: Westminster John Knox, 1994.

Holland, Tom. *Dominion: How the Christian Revolution Remade the World.* New York: Basic, 2019.

Holloway, Richard. *Leaving Alexandria: A Memoir of Faith and Doubt.* Edinburg, Scotland: Canongate, 2012.

Holt, Jim. *Why Does the World Exist: An Existential Detective Story.* New York: W. W. Norton, 2012.

Hossenfelder, Susan. *Existential Physics: A Scientist's Guide to Life's Biggest Questions.* New York: Viking, 2022.

Ignatieff, Michael. *Human Rights as Politics and Idolatry.* Edited by Amy Gutman. Princeton: Princeton University Press, 2001.

Isherwood, Lisa, and Dirk von der Horst. "Normativity and Transgression." In *Contemporary Theological Approaches to Sexuality*, edited by Lisa Isherwood and Dirk von der Horst, 3–22. New York: Routledge, 2018.

———, eds. *Contemporary Theological Approaches to Sexuality.* New York: Routledge, 2018.

James, William. *The Varieties of Religious Experience.* York: Routledge, 2008.

Joas, Hans. *The Sacredness of the Person: A New Genealogy of Human Rights.* Washington, DC: Georgetown University Press, 2013.

Johnson, Denis. *Jesus' Son: Stories.* New York: Farrar, Straus and Giroux, 1992.

Julian of Norwich. *Julian of Norwich: The Showings: Uncovering the Face of the Feminine in Revelations of Divine Love.* Translated by Mirabai Starr. Charlottesville, VA: Hampton Roads, 2022.

Kahn, Paul W. *Out of Eden.* Princeton: Princeton University Press, 2007.

Kangas, David. "Dangerous Joy: Marguerite Porete's Good-bye to the Virtues." *Journal of Religion* 91 (2011) 299–319.

———. *Errant Affirmations: On the Philosophical Meaning of Kierkegaard's Religious Discourses.* London: Bloomsbury, 2018.

Kant, Immanuel. "Idea for a Universal History from a Cosmopolitan Point of View." Sixth Thesis. Quoted in *Kant's Idea for a Universal History: A Critical Guide*, edited by Améilie Oksenberg Rorty, 18–19. Cambridge: Cambridge University Press, 2012.

Keating, Thomas. *Invitation to Love: The Way of Christian Contemplation.* London: Bloomsbury, 2011.

Keen, Sam. "A Conversation with Ernest Becker." *The Ernest Becker Reader.* Edited by Daniel Liechty. Seattle: University of Washington Press, 2005.

Kierkegaard, Soren. *Concluding Unscientific Postscript.* Translated by David Swenson and Walter Lowrie. Princeton: Princeton University Press, 1941.

———. *Eighteen Upbuilding Discourses: Kierkegaard's Writings*. Vol. 5. Translated by Howard V. Hong and Edna H. Hong. Princeton: Princeton University Press, 1992.
———. *Either / Or*. Vol. 1. Translated by Howard V. Hong and Edna H. Hong. Princeton: Princeton University Press, 1987.
———. *Fear and Trembling*. Translated by Alastair Hannay. New York: Penguin, 2006.
———. *Fear and Trembling / Repetition*. Edited and translated by Howard V. Hong and Edna H. Hong. Princeton: Princeton University Press, 1983.
———. *For Self-Examination and Judge for Yourself*. Translated by Howard V. Hong and Edna H. Hong. Princeton: Princeton University Press, 1990.
———. *Journals and Papers*. Translated by Howard V. Hong and Edna H. Hong with Gregor Malantschuk. 7 vols. Bloomington: Indiana University Press, 1967–78.
———. *The Point of View for My Work as an Author*. Translated by Walter Lowrie. New York: Harper & Row, 1962.
———. *The Sickness Unto Death*. Translation by Bruce H. Kirmmse. New York: W. W. Norton, 2023.
———. *Three Discourses on Imagined Occasions*. Translated by Howard V. Hong and Edna Hong. Princeton: Princeton University Press, 1993.
———. *Two Ages: The Age of Revolution and the Present Age*. Translated by Howard V. Hong and Edna Hong. Princeton: Princeton University Press, 1978.
———. *Works of Love*. Edited and translated by Howard V. Hong and Edna H. Hong. Princeton: Princeton University Press, 1995.
King, Martin Luther, Jr. "I Have a Dream." In *Norton Anthology of World Religions: Christianity*, edited by Jack Miles, 624–28. New York: Norton, 2015.
Klee, Paul. *Schöpferisiche Konfession*. Berlin: E. Reiss, 1920.
Kline, Peter. *Passion for Nothing: Kierkegaard's Apophatic Theology*. Minneapolis: Fortress, 2007.
Kovel, Joel. *History and Spirit: An Inquiry into the Philosophy of Liberation*. Boston: Beacon, 1991.
Kurzweil, Ray. *The Singularity Is Near: When Human Beings Transcend Biology*. New York: Viking, 2005.
Lamott, Anne. *Help, Thanks, Wow: The Three Essential Prayers*. New York: Riverhead, 2012.
Larkin, Philip. *Collected Poems*. Edited by Anthony Thwaite. New York: Farrar, Straus, and Giroux, 2003.
Levertov, Denise. "Of Being." Published in *Oblique Prayers* (1984) and in *Collected Poems*, edited by Paul A. Lacey and Anne Dewey, 733–34. New York: New Directions, 2013.
———. "Variation and Reflection on a Theme by Rilke." Published in *Breathing the Water* (1987) and in *Collected Poems*, edited by Paul A. Lacey and Anne Dewey, 779–80. New York: New Directions, 2013.

Bibliography

Liechty, Daniel. "Introduction." In *The Ernest Becker Reader*, edited by Daniel Lietchty, 11–23. Seattle: University of Washington Press and The Ernest Becker Foundation, 2005.

Loy, David. *Lack and Transcendence: The Problem of Death and Life in Psychotherapy, Existentialism, and Buddhism*. Somerville, MA: Wisdom, 2018.

Malick, Terrence, dir. *A Hidden Life*. Fox Searchlight Pictures, Elizabeth Bay Productions, 2019.

Marino, Gordon. "Foreword." In *Kierkegaard and Political Theology*, edited by Roberto Sirvent and Silas Morgan, xiii–xv. Eugene, OR: Pickwick, 2018.

Martin, David. *Art and the Religious Experience: The Language of the Sacred*. Cranbury, NJ: Associated University Presses, 1972.

Marx, Karl. "Contribution to the Critique of Hegel's *Philosophy of Right*: Introduction." In *The Marx-Engels Reader*, edited by Robert C. Tucker, 53–65. New York: Norton, 1978.

McCabe, Herbert. "The Class Struggle and Christian Love." In *God Matters*, 182–98. London: Continuum, 1987.

McCarraher, Eugene. *The Enchantments of Mammon: How Capitalism Became the Religion of Modernity*. Cambridge: Harvard University Press, 2019.

McFague, Sallie. *Speaking in Parables*. Minneapolis: Fortress, 2000.

Melville, Herman. "Bartleby the Scrivener." In *The Piazza Tales and Other Prose Pieces: 1839-1860*, edited by G. Thomas Tanselle et al., 13–45. Evanston: Northwestern University Press and Newberry Library, 1987.

———. "The Encantadas or Enchanted Isles." In *Great Short Works of Herman Melville*, 98–150. New York: Harper & Row, 1969.

———. *Mardi: and a Voyage Thither*. Evanston: Northwestern University Press and Newberry Library, 1970.

Merton, Thomas. *Conjectures of a Guilty Bystander*. New York: Doubleday, 1989.

———. *New Seeds of Contemplation*. New York: New Directions, 1961.

Moslener, Sara. "Sexual Renunciation in Christian History and Theology." In *Contemporary Theological Approaches to Sexuality*, edited by Lisa Isherwood and Dirk von der Horst, 90–101. New York: Routledge, 2018.

Nabokov, Vladimir. *Speak, Memory*. New York: Alfred A. Knopf, 1999.

Nietzsche, Friedrich. *Beyond Good and Evil*. New York: Penguin Classics, 2003.

———. *Twilight of the Gods and the Anti-Christ*. Translated by R. J. Hollingdale. London: Penguin, 1968.

O'Connor, Flannery. "Parker's Back." In *The Complete Stories*, 510–30. New York: Farrar, Straus, and Giroux, 1971.

Osborn, Ronald E. *Humanism and the Death of God: Searching for the Good After Darwin, Marx, and Nietzsche*. Oxford: Oxford University Press, 2017.

Pascal, Blaise. *Pensées*. Translated by William Finlayon Trotter. New York: Dutton, 1958.

Peppiatt, Lucy. *The Imago Dei: Humanity Made in the Image of God*. Eugene, OR: Cascade, 2022.

BIBLIOGRAPHY

Pericles. "Funeral Oration." In *The Landmark Thucydides*, edited by Robert B. Strassler. New York: Free Press, 1996.

Picasso, Pablo. *Picasso Says*. Edited by Hélène Parlmelin. London: Allen & Unwin, 1969.

Porete, Marguerite. *The Mirror of Simple Souls*. Translated by Ellen Babinsky. New York: Paulist, 1998.

Ricoeur, Paul. *Symbolism of Evil*. Translation by Emerson Buchanan. Boston: Beacon, 1967.

———. *Time and Narrative*. Vol. 1. Translated by Kathleen McLaughlin and David Pellauer. Chicago: University of Chicago Press, 1984.

Rieger, Joerg. *Theology in the Capitalocene: Ecology, Identity, Class, and Solidarity*. Minneapolis: Fortress, 2022.

Rilke, Rainer Maria. *Duino Elegies and Sonnets to Orpheus*. Translated by A. Poulin, Jr. Boston: Houghton Mifflin, 1977.

Robinette, Brian D. *The Difference Nothing Makes: Creation, Christ, Contemplation*. Notre Dame: University of Notre Dame Press, 2023.

Roethke, Theodore. "In a Dark Time." In *Collected Poems*, 116–17. New York: Penguin Random House, 1965.

Rohr, Richard. "From Innocence to Knowledge." Center for Action and Contemplation, August 11, 2020. https://cac.org/daily-meditations/from-innocence-to-knowledge-2020-08-11/.

———. *The Universal Christ*. Colorado Springs, CO: Convergent, 2021.

Ross, Alex. "Nietzsche's Eternal Return." *The New Yorker*, October 14, 2019. https://www.newyorker.com/magazine/2019/10/14/nietzsches-eternal-return.

Roth, Philip. *The Dying Animal*. New York: Vintage, 2001.

Samuelson, Scott. *Seven Ways of Looking at Pointless Suffering: What Philosophy Can Tell Us about the Hardest Mystery of All*. Chicago: University of Chicago Press, 2018.

Sartre, Jean-Paul. *Being and Nothingness: A Phenomenological Essay on Ontology*. New York: Washington Square, 1966.

Schleiermacher, Friedrich. *On Religion: Speeches to Its Cultured Despisers*. Edited by Richard Crouter. Cambridge: Cambridge University Press, 1996.

Sells, Michael A. *Mystical Languages of Unsaying*. Chicago: University of Chicago Press, 1994.

Shaw, George Bernard. "The Rabid Watchdogs of Liberty." In *Pygmalion and Three Other Plays*, 30–38. New York: Barnes & Noble, 2004.

Smith, Huston. *The World's Religions*. New York: HarperCollins, 1991.

Sölle, Dorothee. *The Silent Cry: Mysticism and Resistance*. Translation by Barbara and Martin Rumscheidt. Minneapolis: Fortress, 2001.

———. *Thinking About God: An Introduction to Theology*. London: SCM, 1991.

Solomon, Sheldon, et al. *In the Wake of 9/11: The Psychology of Terror*. Washington, DC: American Psychological Association, 2003.

———. *The Worm at the Core: On the Role of Death in Life*. New York: Random House, 2015.

Bibliography

Stevens, Wallace. *The Collected Poems of Wallace Stevens*. New York: Alfred A. Knopf, 2005.
Taylor, Charles. *A Secular Age*. Cambridge: Harvard University Press, 2007.
Taylor, Mark C., et al. *Religion and the Human Image*. Englewood Cliffs, NJ: Prentice-Hall, 1997.
Thucydides. *History of the Peloponnesian War*. Translated by Rex Warner. Penguin Classics, 1972.
Tillich, Paul. *The Courage to Be*. New Haven: Yale University Press, 1952.
———. "The Escape from God." In *The Shaking of the Foundations*, 38–51. New York: Charles Scribner's Sons, 1948.
———. *The Eternal Now*. New York: Charles Scribner's Sons, 1963.
———. *A History of Christian Thought*. Edited by Carl E. Braaten. New York: Simon & Schuster, 1967.
———. "Love Is Stronger Than Death." In *The New Being*, 170–74. Lincoln: University of Nebraska Press, 2005.
———. *The Shaking of the Foundations*. New York: Charles Scribner's Sons, 1948.
———. *Systematic Theology*. Vol. 1. Chicago: University of Chicago Press, 1951.
———. *Systematic Theology*. Vol. 2. Chicago: University of Chicago Press, 1957.
———. *The World Situation*. Minneapolis: Fortress, 1965.
Tolstaya, Katya, and Frank Bestebreurtje. "Furthering the Dialogue between Religious Studies and Theology: An Apophatic Approach as a Heuristic Tool for Methodological Agnosticism." *Journal of the American Academy of Religion* 89 (2021) 469–505.
Tracy, David. *Filaments: Theological Profiles: Selected Essays*. Vol. 2. Chicago: University of Chicago Press, 2020.
Veninga, Jennifer Elisa. "Loving the Ones We See: Kierkegaard's Neighbor-Love and the Politics of Pluralism." In *Kierkegaard and Political Theology*, edited by Roberto Sirvent and Silas Morgan. Eugene, OR: Pickwick, 2018.
Wallace, David Foster. "This Is Water." Transcription of 2005 Commencement Address at Kenyon College. https://web.ics.purdue.edu/~drkelly/DFWKenyonAddress2005.pdf.
Walsh, David. *The Modern Philosophical Revolution: The Luminosity of Existence*. Cambridge: Cambridge University Press, 2008.
Warhol, Andy. Poster for 1968 retrospective at the Moderna Museet in Stockholm, Sweden as reported by Blake Gopnik. *Warhol*. New York: Harper Collins, 2020.
Watts, Michael. *Kierkegaard*. Oxford: One World, 2003.
Weil, Simone. "Human Personality." In *The Simone Weil Reader*, edited by George A. Panichas, 310–20. Mt. Kisko, NY: Moyer Bell, 1977.
West, Cornel. "Justice Is What Love Looks Like in Public." Sermon at Howard University. www.youtube.com/watch?v=nGqP7S_WO60.
Williams, William Carlos. *Pictures from Breughel and Other Poems*. New York: New Directions, 1967.

BIBLIOGRAPHY

Wiman, Christian. *Every Riven Thing: Poems.* New York: Farrar, Straus and Giroux, 2010.

Wirzba, Norman. *Way of Love: Recovering the Heart of Christianity.* New York: Harper Collins, 2016.

Woolf, Virginia. *Mrs. Dalloway.* New York: Harcourt Brace Jovanovich, 1981.

Yeats, William Butler. "Byzantium." In *Selected Poems and Two Plays of William Butler Yeats*, edited M. L. Rosenthal, 32–33. New York: Macmillan, 1962.

Author Index

Arendt, Hannah, 90
Aristotle, 24
Armstrong, Karen, 8
Aroosi, Jamie, 61
Aspray, Barnabas, 85
Augustine, 78

Baard, Rachel Sophia, 38
Backhouse, Stephen, 96
Baldwin, James, 83–84
Bass, Diana Butler, 94
Bates, Harvey, 84
Beal, Timothy, 4, 72
Beck, Richard, 52
Becker, Ernest, xv, xx, 57, 84–85
Beckett, Samuel, 98
Biale, David, 44
Blake, William, 40, 48
Bloch, Ernest, 82
Bolz-Weber, Nadia, 37–38
Borg, Marcus, 36, 67
Brown, David, 101
Brueggemann, Walter, 71
Buber, Martin, 1
Bukowski, Charles, xiii

Calvin, John, 22
Campbell, Joseph, 16
Carroll, James, 92
Carse, James P., 7, 100
Case, Anne, 5
Champion, James, 68

Chilton, Bruce, 68
Christie, Douglas E., 82
Churchland, Patricia S., 55
Clarke, Santhinatha, 51
Cohen, Leonard, 43
Coleridge, Samuel Taylor, 17
Crossan, John Dominic, 15, 67, 69–70, 89, 100
Crossan, Sara, 89

Darwin, Charles, 20
Deaton, Angus, 5
Dickinson, Emily, 10
Dodd, C. H., 68
Dorrien, Gary, 15
Dostoevsky, Fyodor, 42–43
Dowling, David, 18

Eagleton, Terry, 10
Eckhart, Meister, 1, 6
Einstein, Albert, 19
Eliade, Mircea, 15
Epicurus, 62

Farley, Wendy, 35, 47, 95
Faulkner, William, 18
Fowles, John, 8
Franke, William, 6, 17, 35
Frye, Northrop, 15, 57

Gander, Forrest, 98
Garff, Joakim, 96

Author Index

Garrels, Scott, 91
Gillespie, Michael Allen, 33, 58
Girard, Rene, 86–89
Gopnik, Blake, 53
Gordon, Mary, 102
Greenberg, Jeff, xviii, 13–14, 90
Greene, Brian, 52, 84

Hanh, Thich Nhat, 99
Hall, Douglas John, 46
Hall, Shannon, 72
Hammarskjöld, Dag, xx
Harries, Richard, 40
Havel, Vaclav, 45
Haven, Cynthia L., 88, 90–91
Hawthorne, Hawthorne, 100
Hedges, Chris, 38
Hegel, Georg W. F., xix
Heim, S. Mark, 88
Heschel, Abraham J., 3
Hesla, David, 23–24
Hodgson, Peter C., 30, 77
Holland, Tom, 1
Holloway, Richard, 37–38
Holt, Jim, 79–80
Hopps, Gavin, 101
Hossenfelder, Susan, 80

Ignatieff, Michael, 53–54
Isherwood, Lisa, 36

James, William, 57
Joas, Hans, 53
Johnson, Denis, 74
Julian of Norwich, 95

Kahn, Paul W., 30
Kangas, David, 34, 74
Kant, Immanuel, 22
Keating, Thomas, 81
Keen, Sam, 84
Kierkegaard, Soren, 39, 48, 56, 58–65
King, Martin Luther, 3
Klee, Paul, 18

Kline, Peter, 63
Kovel, Joel, 21
Kurzweil, Ray, 20

Lamott, Anne, 99
Larkin, Philip, 62
Levertov, Denise, 48, 102
Liechty, Daniel, 109
Loy, David, 27–28

Malick, Terrence, 93
Marino, Gordon, 65
Martin, David, 18
Marx, Karl, 41
McCabe, Herbert, 66
McCarraher, Eugene, 56
McFague, Sallie, 67
Melville, Herman, 1, 21, 42
Merton, Thomas, 45, 82

Nabokov, Vladimir, xiii
Nietzsche, Friedrich, 35, 54–55

O'Connor, Flannery, 75
Osborn, Ronald E., xx, 53, 93

Pascal, Blaise, 48
Peppiatt, Lucy, 53
Pericles, 25
Picasso, Pablo, 19
Porete, Marguerite, 35, 82
Pyszczynski, Tom, xviii, 13–14, 90

Ricoeur, Paul, 37, 42, 44
Rieger, Joerg, 66
Rilke, Rainer Maria, 102
Robinette, Brian D., 78, 80 86
Roethke, Theodore, 97
Rohr, Richard, 29, 67
Ross, Alex, 55
Roth, Philip, xiv

Samuelson, Scott, 34, 54–55, 97
Sartre, Jean-Paul, 40
Schleiermacher, Friedrich, 52

Author Index

Sells, Michael A., 1
Shaw, George Bernard, xv
Smith, Huston, 26
Sölle, Dorothee, 8, 29
Solomon, Sheldon, xviii, 13–14, 90
Stevens, Wallace, 75

Taylor, Barbara Brown, 89
Taylor, Charles, xvi, 41, 56
Taylor, Mark C., 26
Thucydides, 25
Tillich, Paul, xvii–xviii, 11, 16, 32, 34, 46–47, 63, 97
Tolstaya, Katya, 76
Tracy, David, 75

Veninga, Jennifer Elisa, 64

Wallace, David Foster, 39
Walsh, David, xvii
Warhol, Andy, 53
Watts, Michael, 61–62
Weil, Simone, 9
West, Cornel, 65
Williams, William Carlos, 12
Wiman, Christian, 46
Wirzba, Norman, 66
Woolf, Virginia, 75

Yeats, William Butler, 16

www.ingramcontent.com/pod-product-compliance
Lightning Source LLC
Chambersburg PA
CBHW020856160426
43192CB00007B/952